TRACES Mapping a Journey in Textiles

Gregg Museum of Art & Design, North Carolina State University, Raleigh NC   January 20 - May 14, 2011

cover: Marian Bijlenga, detail: *Palimpsest 1*, 2007, detail left: Carol Ann Carter, *Solo Moments*, 2010, back cover: Clare Verstegen, *Safety Measures*, 2009

As with many projects, the seed is planted long before the idea germinates. This is true of *Traces: Mapping a Journey in Textiles*. The first time I met Barbara Lee Smith was in 1994. She was visiting the Gregg Museum of Art & Design (then known as the Visual Art Center) in connection with the exhibition, *Celebrating the Stitch*, a result of her well-received and much-heralded book by the same name. The exhibition opened Thursday, January 20, 1994, and Smith spoke the following Friday afternoon. I was deep into my doctoral studies, exploring how women tell their history, and my focus on journals had me reading the work of May Sarton. One chapter in Sarton's book, *Writings on Writing,* seemed particularly important. It was on revision as creation. I recommended this chapter to Smith and this became my first correspondence with her. Smith graciously replied saying that she enjoyed Sarton's comments about "getting in in order to get out." Sarton was a favorite of hers as well. Smith recognized how hard it is to keep from getting too tangled in one's own work. I have thought about that phrase "getting in … " as I have worked on this exhibition.

When I joined the Gregg as curator in 2002, I started seeing Barbara Lee Smith's name come across my desk. I enjoyed reading her book reviews and quickly added these titles to my library. Two of the most important were Lenore Tawney's *Signs on the Wind*, which focused on postcard collages, and Twyla Tharp's book, *The Creative Habit: Learn It and Use It for Life*. I had seen Tawney's exhibition at the Renwick Gallery, part of the Smithsonian Institution National Museum of American Art, and it still counts as one of my favorite installations. While the scope of Tawney's work in the exhibition took my breath away, it was her postcard collages that intrigued me the most. The layering aspect of collage helps me to understand the artist's process. And as a former struggling modern dancer, I was well acquainted with Twyla Tharp and jumped at a chance to step inside her creative mind.

In fact, creativity is another connection I have with Smith. At the invitation of NC State's College of Textiles in early 2004, Smith came for a meeting that delved into creativity and technology. We began another cycle of e-mail exchanges about the creative process, since I teach *Creativity in Management*, a course in the MBA program at NC State. In 2006, Smith's handsome monograph catalog piqued my interest and I began to think about a major exhibition that would focus on textiles. Back in 1992, the Gregg Museum opened in its new space with a textile exhibition, *The New Narrative: Contemporary Fiber Art*, guest curated by Nancy Corwin. Nine artists from around the United States displayed their work in this exhibition. Given the importance of textiles to North Carolina, it seemed the perfect time to once again explore the world of fibers.

In early 2008 I asked Smith to guest curate an exhibition that would open at the Gregg in January 2011. She would determine the theme, and *Traces: Mapping a Journey in Textiles* has unfolded over the past three years. Twelve artists from throughout the United States, Canada and the Netherlands comprise this show that serves as a bookend to the earlier exhibition, *The New Narrative*.

In conjunction with the Gregg Museum, I have organized a symposium, *Trace Evidence,* that will take place March 24-26, 2011. Its purpose is to explore thoughts of how textiles serve as an accessible and suitable medium for communicating the interconnected tracings of the paths we travel. There will be an artists' reception, panel discussions, a keynote address by Dr. Glenn Adamson, deputy head of research and head of graduate studies, Victoria and Albert Museum; and a lunch

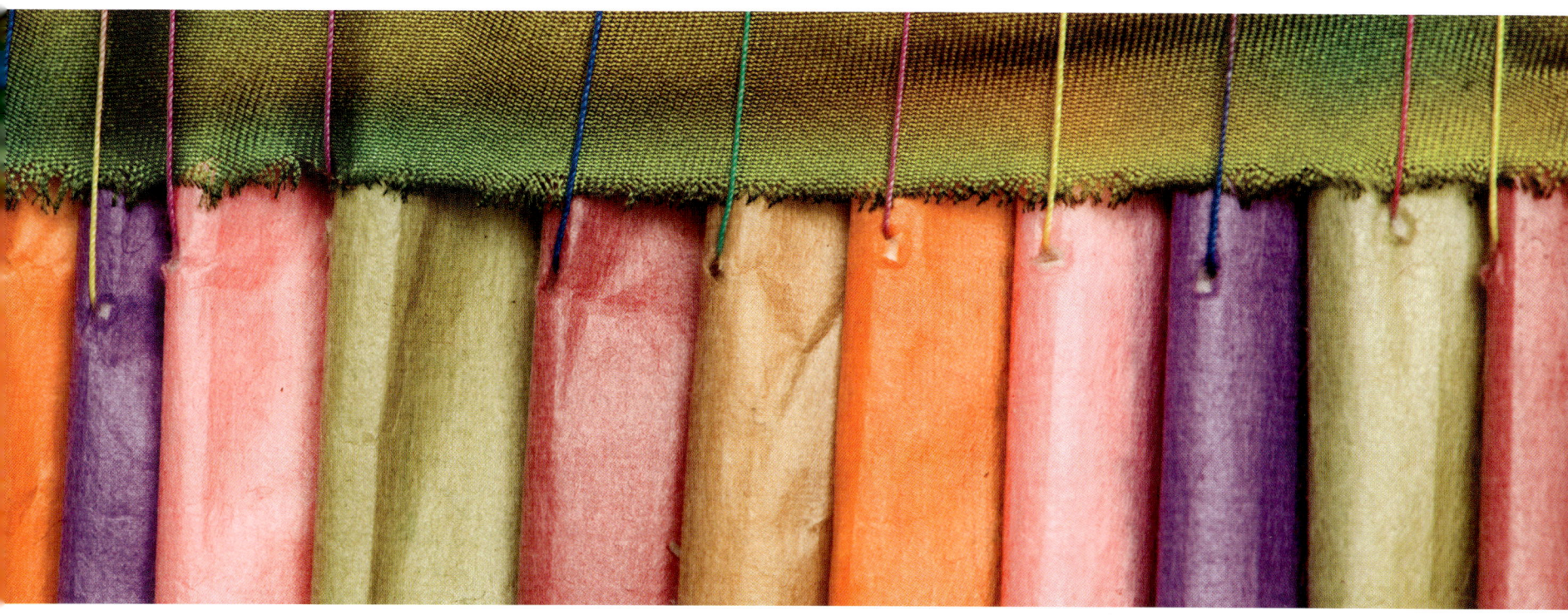

detail: Gail Rieke, *Blaze of Glory/Japan and Korea 2007-2009*

address by Dr. Blanton Godfrey, Dean, NCSU College of Textiles. Panels will focus on the creative community, moving into new terrain, challenging assumptions, and the artist and the environment. Noted textile artists and College of Design faculty Susan Brandeis, Vita Plume and Jan-Ru Wan will serve as panelists together with artists in the *Traces* exhibition. In addition to the Gregg's exhibition, a number of institutions throughout the Raleigh area are hosting textile exhibitions during the symposium.

I would like to thank the staff of the Gregg Museum as well as the catalog editor Carol Douglas, designer Jessie Brinkley and photographer David Ramsey. I would also like to thank Peter Turchi for his willingness to cast a writer's eye on the textiles in this exhibition. His essay helps to layer yet another meaning to this work. Genevieve Garland of NC State's Nonwovens Institute kept up a steady interest in what we were doing. To Barbara Lee Smith and her family, my thanks for her leadership and thoughtfulness as she developed this exhibition. To the students of NC State — thank you. You are the ones who make it possible to do what we do.

— *Lynn Jones Ennis,* Associate Director and Curator of the Collection

The Age of String

Ce n'est pas le temps qui passe, mais nous. — Ferdinand Cheval[1]

At some point long after our ancestors finally came down out of the trees, stood up, looked around, and began scrounging for things to eat — and started making gear to help them accomplish that endless task — they entered what scholars millennia later would term the Paleolithic Period, a greekified way of saying "the Old Stone Age." Centuries rolled by and this slowly and imperceptibly segued into the Meso- and Neolithic Periods (or Middle and New Stone Ages) before the Ages of Bronze and Iron came along.

All these ages were named (in the 1860s) for the relatively limited range of objects that had proved tough enough to withstand lying forgotten in damp caves or buried under layers of sediment for thousands of European winters before some amateur collector or archaeologist happened along to pick them up and take them home. Due to the unrelenting processes of time — the physical and chemical actions of erosion and decay — nearly all traces of the journey down through time from the distant past were reduced to only the hardest, heaviest, and most impervious of materials. Of all the other artificial accouterments of early human life, almost the only items to resist rot, insects and weathering long enough to be rediscovered were stone axes, stone-tipped spears and arrows, and the blades of ancient swords and daggers.

But there was more to the Stone Ages than stones. Anthropologist Elizabeth Fisher points out that nearly all the hunter-gatherer societies that survived into recent times depended almost wholly on *gathering*, i.e., that they mostly went out looking for fruits, nuts, seeds and roots, and that even the majority of the animal protein they hauled home was trapped, snared, netted or caught with hook and line — while only comparatively rarely did they dare risk hunting with axes, spears or arrows. She proposes that rather than something made of stone for chopping, slashing, bashing or penetrating, "the first cultural device was probably a recipient … a container to hold gathered products [or] some kind of sling or net carrier." Objects made of fibers, in other words, almost certainly predated any tools made of stone.[2]

But first in time doesn't mean longest-lasting. Other than a few widely-scattered fragments of plaited leaves or twisted strands of hair left in frozen tundra, or perhaps some faint imprints of twilled material left on fire-hardened clay and a few hanks of string preserved in desert sands, all those earliest, fiber-made objects were as ephemeral (and now as lost) as the chants and laughter of the people who made them, the vast majority of whom were likely female. To argue, however, that because the objects were short-lived, they were insignificant, would be just as absurd as saying that our maternal ancestors weren't important because they are no longer with us. The String Age may never have been named, but just as we still carry the genes of our ancient mothers, the traces of those long-lost fibers wind through everything we are and do today.

Traces: Mapping a Journey in Textiles, presents further proof of the false disconnect between evanescence and significance. For a few months, a gathering of ephemeral objects (made mostly of short-lived stuff like threads, paper, fish scales, leaves, roots, silk or horsehair), which have been skillfully netted up from a mixed bag of artists scattered across three countries, is woven into a space where we — temporary tenants on this planet ourselves — have a chance to see, enjoy, and respond to them.[3] Thanks to fellow fiber artist Barbara Lee Smith, who curated the choice of artists and objects, and Gregg Museum Associate Director Lynn Ennis, who curated the concurrent show of Smith's work and organized the exhibitions and accompanying symposium, we've all been offered a brief period in which to reflect once again on how fleeting are most of the most beautiful things in life — think of sunsets, falling stars, lovers' smiles, innocence — and to remind ourselves how the very fact that they don't last forever is what, in large measure, makes them mean as much as they do.

— *Roger Manley*, Director

[1] "It is not time that passes, but us." Inscription on a sundial at the Palais Idéal visionary art environment built by the postman Ferdinand Cheval in Hautrives, France

[2] Fisher, Elizabeth. 1979. *Women's Creation: Sexual Evolution and the Shaping of Society.* Garden City, NY: Anchor Press/Doubleday. The wisdom of this chronology is intuitively embedded in that age-old deciding game in which paper (i.e., fiber) beats rock (bashing tool), and rock beats scissors (refined cutting tools). Since cutting tools made refining fibers easier, scissors in turn beat paper, completing the circle. But no one would argue that stone knives preceded raw stones, so fibers logically win the timeline race.

[3] In a gallery space which itself will soon be gone forever too, when the Talley Center is gutted and renovated and the Gregg Museum moves across campus to occupy its first stand-alone facility!

detail opposite: Devorah Sperber, *After Grant Wood, American Gothic 2*, 2006

Traces: An Invitation

We do this: we move into an apartment, a house, a room, an office, and we make it ours. We bring the things we use, the things we need, but also photographs, mementos, and objects that, no matter how ordinary, how unremarkable they might seem to others, carry meaning for us. Reminders of where we've been, and of who and where we want to be. From where I sit, I can see a ceramic candleholder made by a long-deceased relative, a hand-carved bowl brought home from South Africa, a trophy topped by a replica Good Humor ice cream truck, four prints made by an artist friend, another brought from Germany in a backpack, a piece of functional sculpture my wife and I bought ourselves for our anniversary, a pressed flower from British Columbia, a rug bought from a relative of a famous pool player, and a teapot in the shape of a desk, acquired in England long ago. This room I'm in, like your rooms — like this exhibition — holds a cluster of private narratives.

Traces: Mapping a Journey in Textiles is a wide-ranging collection by diverse artists working independently. We encounter an exhibit like this one on many levels, including the aesthetic (*That's beautiful!* if the textures, shapes, and composition give us pleasure; *They call that art?* if they leave us cold), the intellectual (we recognize *This is a quilt; that's a scrap of an old check,* and we think, *This exhibit has a theme — how does each piece relate to it?*), the emotional, the pragmatic (*How much does that cost? That would never fit in our house*), the egotistical (*I could do that!*), and the personal (*My grandmother made me one of those*).

The personal.

One of my earliest memories is of sitting on the floor of the living room of the house I grew up in as my sister, four and a half years older, patiently showed me how to use a square metal frame. The frame had upward-projecting teeth, and she carefully looped brightly colored elasticized cloth bands from tooth to opposite tooth, parallel to one another. When she finished in one direction, she chose more bands from a bag, then patiently wove them over and under, perpendicular to the first set.

The result: a decorative and perfectly functional potholder. My introduction to fiber arts.

One of the earliest meanings of the word "trace" is "to make a plan or diagram."

Curiously, another meaning might seem to be the opposite: "to follow, or pursue." We trace a plan of our own, or we follow in another's footsteps. Or, more often, we believe we're doing one, but we're also doing the other.

We pursue the truth.

We pursue meaning.

We pursue our dreams.

We pursue understanding, a kind of knowledge that results from making connections.

After nearly twenty years in North Carolina, I now live in the Southwest, in an exotic landscape rich with history. Ruins of cliff dwellings 700 to 900 years old can be found not only at Mesa Verde but at hundreds of other sites, some famous, others virtually unknown. Most people encountering cliff dwellings for the first time ask understandable questions: Why did those people go to the trouble of building homes in a place they'd have to risk their lives to reach? How exactly did they live? What did the geometric patterns on their pottery mean to them? To what extent was the shape and appearance of the things they created determined by the tools and materials at their disposal, and to what extent were they exerting taste, and choice?

And always: what happened? Why did they leave so suddenly, and leave so much behind?

Those questions aren't so different from the ones we pose standing in the confusion of ruins we call the Roman Forum, looking at the remains of an old barn or farmhouse, or contemplating all that's left behind when someone close to us is gone. The difference is, with no written clues, our sense of wonder is even greater. We stare at the pots, the sandals, the petroglyphs, and we imagine our way into their world — a world almost completely unfamiliar and, at the same time, given the presence of pots, sandals, and pictures on the walls, a world not so very different from our own.

In junior high school, for a variety of reasons including but not limited to the fact that my family and I had visited Hawaii, I began wearing Hawaiian shirts to school. These weren't the lightweight, short-sleeve, buttondown shirts that are more or less fashionable these days, but large pieces of brightly dyed cloth with a neckhole. No one I knew in Baltimore, Maryland, was wearing anything like them. My sister made me a few. One of them was pink, with large white flowers. People — friends, teachers, strangers — could not resist comment. Those shirts were extraordinarily powerful. And they were perfect for a shy, awkward teenager, as they both demanded attention and made it possible to hide in plain sight. The shirts were an outrageous costume.

Later, my sister made me other shirts, often from patterned material with a theme — stamps, license plates, baseball gear. On one, the stitching along the yoke traced the outline of a freight train. While she loved (and still loves) to sew, the work never came easy, nothing ever flew together. Patterns refused to lie flat, buttonholes fought back.

Back then, when she made me those shirts, I didn't understand what they meant.

How do we know what someone else considers valuable? For starters, whether it is used or displayed. If it's displayed, how and where. To hang a rug or quilt on the wall, where it cannot be used, is to say: Look at this.

If we follow the advice of veteran museum guides, we walk toward the work that first catches our eye, then cross the room to another work, then re-cross the room to a third, thereby avoiding the fatigue that comes from the museum death march, the dutiful inspection of every object, the reading of every placard. Or we succumb to that march, like pilgrims on a quasi-spiritual mission. Or we follow our companions. However we choose to encounter this work, we trace a path, consciously or not, through what more people than we'll ever know have labored for months to choose and to arrange precisely.

We encounter any single piece on display the way poet and novelist Stephen Dobyns says we encounter anything we read: in the present; in the near past, comparing what we're seeing to what we just saw; in the distant past, comparing what we're seeing to other things we've seen and known; and in the future, anticipating other things we'll see, or even make.

In this way, we constantly chart paths through both time and space.

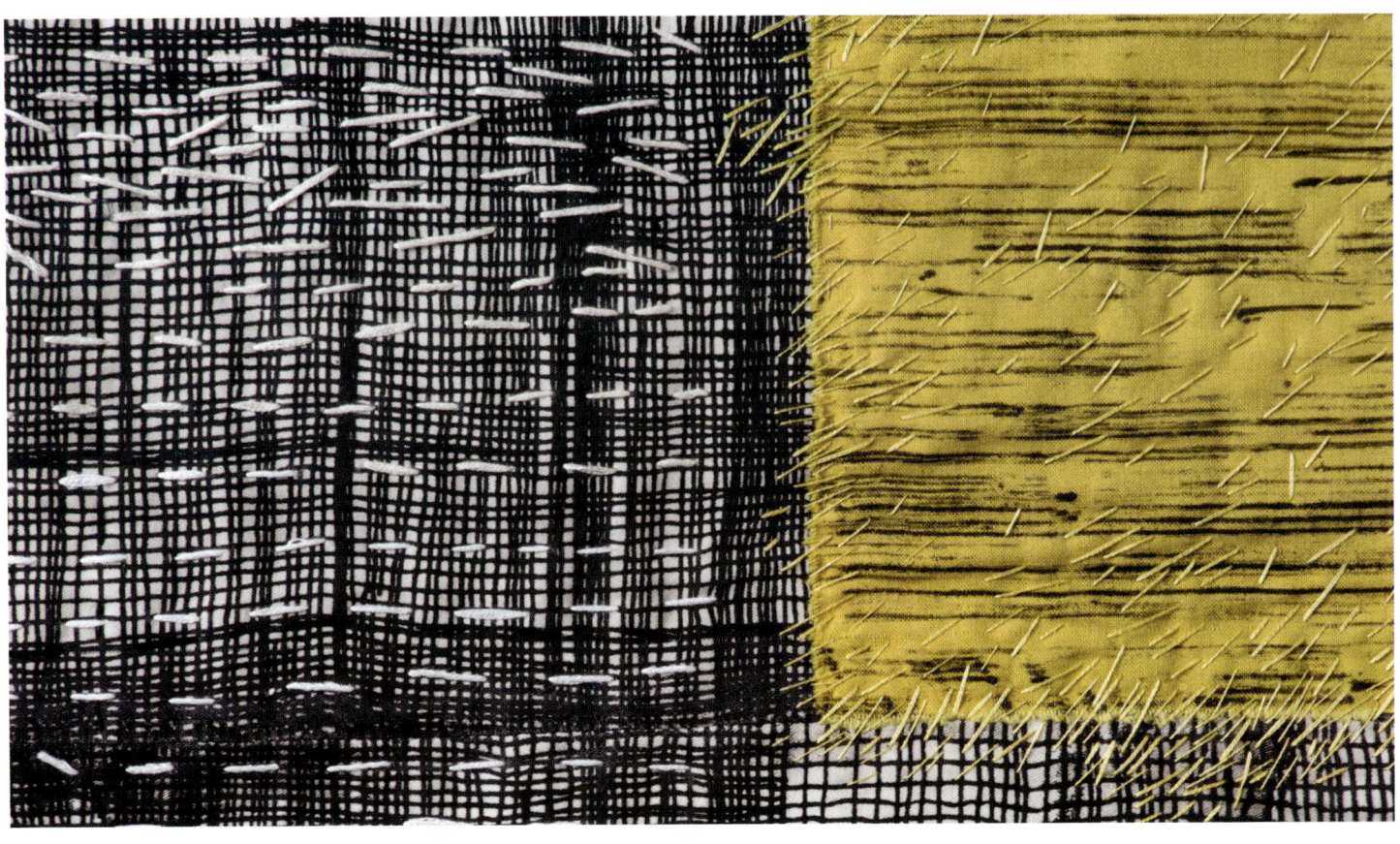

Dorothy Caldwell, detail: *Fjord*, 2010

One morning last spring, my wife and I noticed a trace of something sticky on one of the light fixtures hanging from the ceiling fan on our patio. A few days later, it seemed larger. A few days after that, we could see the nest taking shape.

The final product, about the size of a golf ball, soon contained two jelly-bean-sized hummingbird eggs. A few weeks later, yellow beaks were visible, bits of candy corn. I stood on a chair to inspect the work on display, made of materials light enough for a hummingbird — itself weighing about as much as a dime — to carry: bits of plants, some blue and red thread. Wired into that tiny brain, the knowledge of what would serve the purpose, and how to weave the disparate parts to make something solid and strong enough to support two new lives.

"They make the nest to resemble the plants around them — it's camouflage," a docent at the Arizona-Sonora Desert Museum told us. But of course, bits of the plants around them are also the handiest things to collect. The nest on our patio fan, just a few feet from the table where my wife and I read the paper each morning, contained a short strip of newsprint.

Eventually the young birds outgrew the nest — destroyed it, except for the adhesive ring that had held it firm.

To leave a trace: to make a mark. Before there can be a trace, then, there must be a blank for the trace to be left upon, and some force or being to make it. Some people say those cliff dwellers, the Ancestral Puebloans, formerly called the Anasazi, vanished without a trace, but the pottery and sandals, the canals and mortared walls remind us that is far from the case. Absent from the kivas and cliff dwellings are the people who made them; the things they left behind, the vivid traces of their presence, their lives, makes us feel their absence more profoundly.

Every effective work of art is part puzzle, part mystery. The puzzle is the arrangement of elements that creates a satisfying whole. The interplay of those elements may be immediately apparent to the viewer, but more often our understanding or appreciation of a work grows — expands, develops — as we consider it. The balancing of shapes and colors might act on us subconsciously, and we might never recognize what creates the sensation we feel. The artist, either consciously or through experience and intuition, has discovered an effective arrangement of parts.

But the mystery … in the best work, the artist has no answer for the mystery, but leads us to contemplate it. To offer selected and arranged fragments, to suggest connections, routes, is to leave the work open to the viewer's completion.

For Barbara Lee Smith to select artists, and with them select individual examples of their work for this exhibit, and for the good people of the Gregg Museum of Art & Design to present them this way, is to extend an invitation to us, to roll out the metaphorical carpet.

In Anne Carson's translation of *Agamemnon*, by Aiskhylos, the warrior king is greeted on his return home from war by his wife, Klytaimestra, who for one reason and another intends to kill him. "And now, dear one," she says, "as a special favor to me, I pray you descend from your car without setting foot on the ground." She commands her servants to "strew the ground with fabrics, now!" The wary king resists: "Don't pamper me … don't strew my path with anything at all! You'll draw down envy. That stuff is for gods." When she insists, he says, "As I tread upon these crimson cloths let no evil eye of envy from the gods strike down on me. What a shame to trample the wealth of the house and ruin fabrics worth their weight in silver." The king's instincts are right; "the trampling of many cloths" foreshadows much worse.

More than a century later, kings seem to have lost any scruples about conspicuous consumption. In *Aladdin and the Enchanted Lamp*, Aladdin tells the genie, "I require a carpet of rich brocade, woven with gold … It must be stretched from this palace to the Sultan's, so that Princess Badr-al-Budur may walk upon it without treading the ground."

The princess, the most beautiful woman in the kingdom, should, on her wedding day, trace a path of the finest fabric from her father's house to her husband's. From her past to her future.

Leap to Australia in the 19th century. In Peter Carey's *True History of the Kelly Gang*, Ned Kelly, based on the actual outlaw/hero, recognizes the danger he's in because of a conspicuous display of wealth: "a handsome Constable in a uniform appeared like he were a butler then I seen a mighty Turk rug stretching out before me it were blue and vermilion no one in my family could of imagined such a lovely thing I could not credit I were permitted to walk on it in my boots … I could not predict what bad thing would happen to me here." Putting an object we use every day on display, drawing attention to it as something other than merely functional, can seem odd; but putting art under our feet feels something like sacrilege.

Ned Kelly spent most of his short adult life hiding from enforcers of the law; in Carey's novel, he spends his final days writing, intent on explaining himself.

Two impulses: to disappear without a trace; to leave a trace. The first, while often associated with those who have criminal intent, or missing persons, can also represent a desire for objectivity or perfection: the window perfectly clean, free of watermarks, streaks, thumbprints or dust. The piece of art that draws no attention to its maker, that leaves the viewer to confront the object, as if the artist were nonexistent. The goal: to lead the viewer into an uninterrupted dream.

The second is commonly identified with our desire for immortality, the desire to make our presence known: the gash in the bark of a tree to signify *someone has been here before you*, the flag planted on distant shores (the footprints in the sand of those shores insufficient to satisfy the impulse), the cherished objects we bequeath to others, the influence we hope to have.

While one might initially seem selfless, the other egotistical, in fact both can be borne of a generosity of spirit: not *Look at me!* but *Look at us.* Not *This is what I can do* but *Here: this is for you.*

One of the world's leading dealers of pre-Columbian textiles tells colorful stories about collecting pieces when he was young, going from village to village, home to home. "How did you know what was good from what was mediocre?" I asked. I wondered if he had taken courses, had some sort of informal training, served as an apprentice; he said he hadn't.

Later, he told a story from his childhood, a story about a favorite uncle who took great pride in the suits he wore. "He'd come into the house," the textiles dealer said, "and he'd hold out his sleeve and say, 'Billy, feel the cloth. Feel the cloth!'"

At some point after junior high school — but not long after — my sense of myself, and of who I wanted to be, changed. My sister kept making me brightly patterned shirts.

Decades later, I learned that the business manager of the college where I taught had sewn his daughter's wedding dress. That single piece of information completely changed my sense of him. To make clothing for someone, I understood by then, is an act of devotion.

Trace: a minute and often barely detectable amount or indication.

The artists represented here offer us their work, their vision, public creations embodying fragments of their private narratives. Encountering it without any explanatory prose, we have no way of knowing that one was made in response to the terrorist attacks of 9/11, another was informed by the death of a brother, yet another means to commemorate, through playfully mapping the tiny holes in a wall, a friend's artistic career, the result of years of work pinned in place. Looking at a dress at a yard sale, a shirt in a closet, we might not detect the love of a father for his daughter, of a sister for her brother. But even if, in this work, we recognize only the beauty of colors, the sensual appeal of textures, the interplay of man's geometry and the apparent chaos of blades of grass, the shadow-pattern echoing the pattern of monofilament and horsehair, we suspect communication, we're alert to the presence of another.

This summer, when monsoon winds blew our patio furniture over, we hurriedly took the feeder inside. As soon as the winds slowed — and though the rain continued — hummingbirds flew to exactly where the feeder usually hangs. They hovered; they waited. Obviously, they knew food had been there. Was there evidence, something we can't see or smell? Or was a bit of information, a memory, stored in that miniscule brain? In that brain a map, of sorts, from flower to feeder to flower to nest, a path traced and retraced day after day.

Trace: a mark or line left by something that has passed; a path, trail, or road made by the passage of animals, vehicles, or people.

Every piece an artist creates is the product of what that artist has observed, considered, imagined, lived, and collected. It is both culmination and artifact. And for the true artist, every creation is one more step on a journey with no clear destination … a breadcrumb in a fairy tale, a cairn beside a mountain trail, a sign intended both to guide others and to mark where the explorer has been.

But "guide" is the wrong word. This work doesn't mean simply to carry us along, to deliver us from here to there; neither does it mean simply to reassure us, to confirm what we already knew, or believed, before we saw it. Poet Heather McHugh: "We are creatures of habit: given a blank we can't help trying to fill it in along lines of customary seeing or saying. But the best poetic lines undermine those habits, break the pre- off the -dictable, unsettle the suburbs of your routine sentiments, and rattle the tracks of your trains of thought."

Whenever we choose to encounter art, we have expectations, assumptions about what we might find; and having those assumptions confirmed can be pleasant. But if we're lucky, something we see here puzzles us, possibly even disturbs us, disrupts, refuses to fit neatly with those expectations.

We surround ourselves with meaningful objects and images because they connect us to others and to our own past; also because they draw us out of ourselves, beyond this moment, this place. We journey beyond the familiar to make new discoveries. This is why we came here, to this work: not to be reassured in what we comprehend, what we already grasp, but to be invited to extend our reach.

— *Peter Turchi*

Peter Turchi has co-edited three anthologies and is the award-winning author of five books including, most recently, *Maps of the Imagination: The Writer as Cartographer*. He currently teaches at Arizona State University.

Traces: Mapping a Journey in Textiles

An unfinished sentence.

Pin marks on a wall.

Erasures, outlines, shadows, the imprint of a hand. A sigh.

All are traces: marks as well as markers that indicate a current or past human presence. Traces are suggestions — seductive mysteries for the curious — beckoning some to follow, like blaze-marks, into the woods to begin a journey.

Artists can't resist intriguing leads and they respond, leaving a visual record for all to see. The viewer, in turn, follows the artist's lead in a continuing process of discovery with yet more questions and responses, and even possible action. The painter, Agnes Martin, wrote about this artist/viewer connection in her *Response to Art*:

The cause of the response is not traceable in the work.

An artist cannot and does not prepare for a certain response.

He does not consider the response but simply follows his inspiration.

… The response depends on the conditions of the observer.[1]

As one who traced my way for three years through the selection of artists and art, I hope to add information to this process that will enrich your response to the work in *Traces: Mapping a Journey in Textiles*.

Traces is a timely exhibition. The chosen works extend from 2000 to 2010, and while all times are unique, there were circumstances during the first decade of the 21st century that shook and shrunk our world. We tracked changes as towers fell, icebergs melted and seas rose, volcanoes blew up while economies collapsed. Wars came and went and came again. Despite the shocks, or perhaps because of them, this has been a time for reflection; for re-engagement with beauty; for personal journeys of recovery and discovery. We have come to value our 'place' at home as we reevaluate our 'place' in the world.

These twelve artists explore personal, social and scientific issues. Each visual voice varies, sometimes quiet and spare, sometimes rich with color and fiery energy, tracing a poetic thread through this collection of compositions. We listen to the work, for when our days are filled with the noise of story, fact and image — thanks to the twitter of the Internet — perhaps poetry is our sanest response.

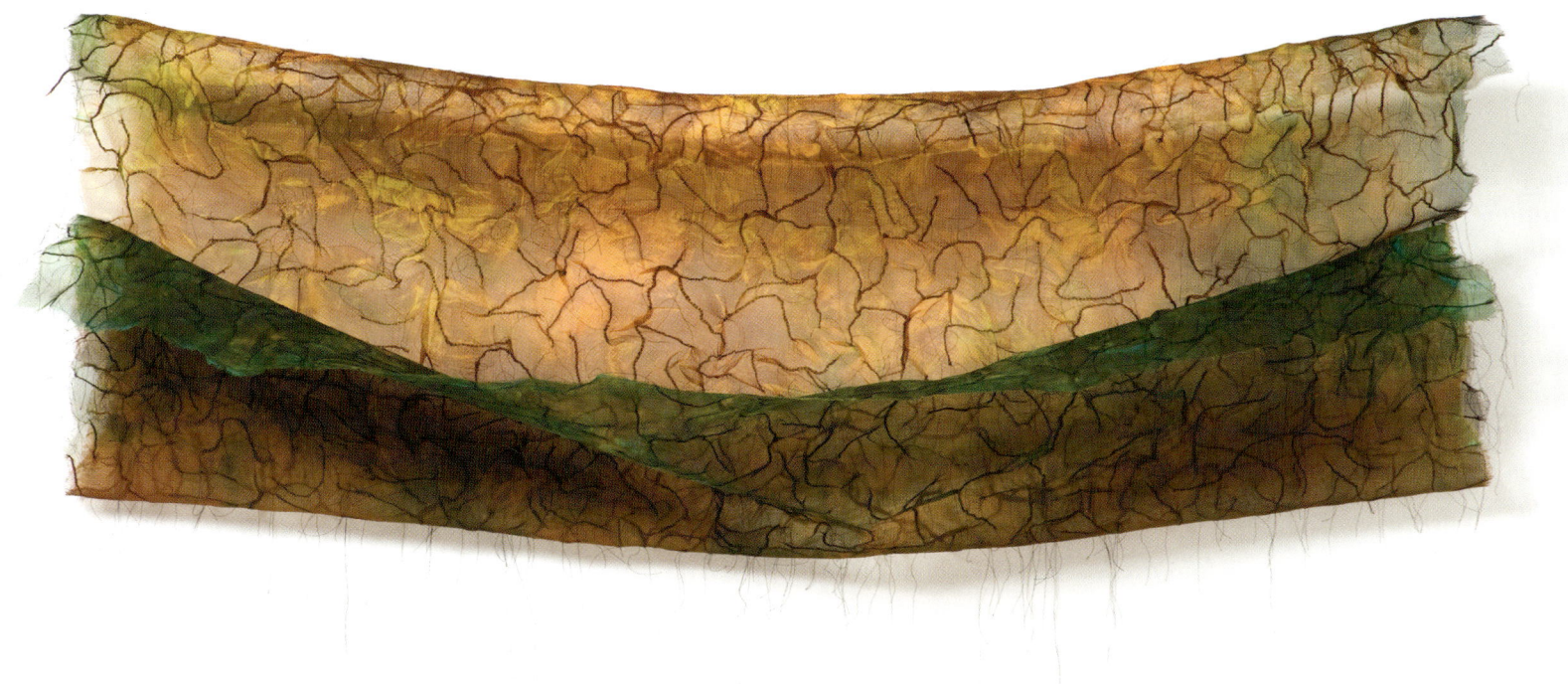

Susan Lordi Marker, *The Field is Sown*, 2010, 30 x 48"

Our time offers an abundance of information and opportunity, and artists trace journeys through a world more accessible than ever before. Other lands and people provide rich fodder for the traveling artist who comes to what is new with discerning eye and an open mind. Unique tools and materials, new technologies and scientific discoveries present themselves for exploration, and artists rise to the challenge.

The present and the future are well represented here, but the tradition of the textile past is also present, forming a foundation upon which much of the work is constructed: assembling, collecting, sewing, ripping, patching, binding, stringing, piercing, mending. The art in *Traces* offers keys to mapping a personal journey, as well as a call to care for our fragile selves and world, and a celebration of the strong threads that bind us together.

— *Barbara Lee Smith,* Guest Curator

[1] Martin, Agnes. *Writings*. Catalog published to accompany the exhibition, *Agnes Martin: Paintings and Works on Paper*, 1960-1989, Kunstmuseum Winterthur, Switzerland, 1992.

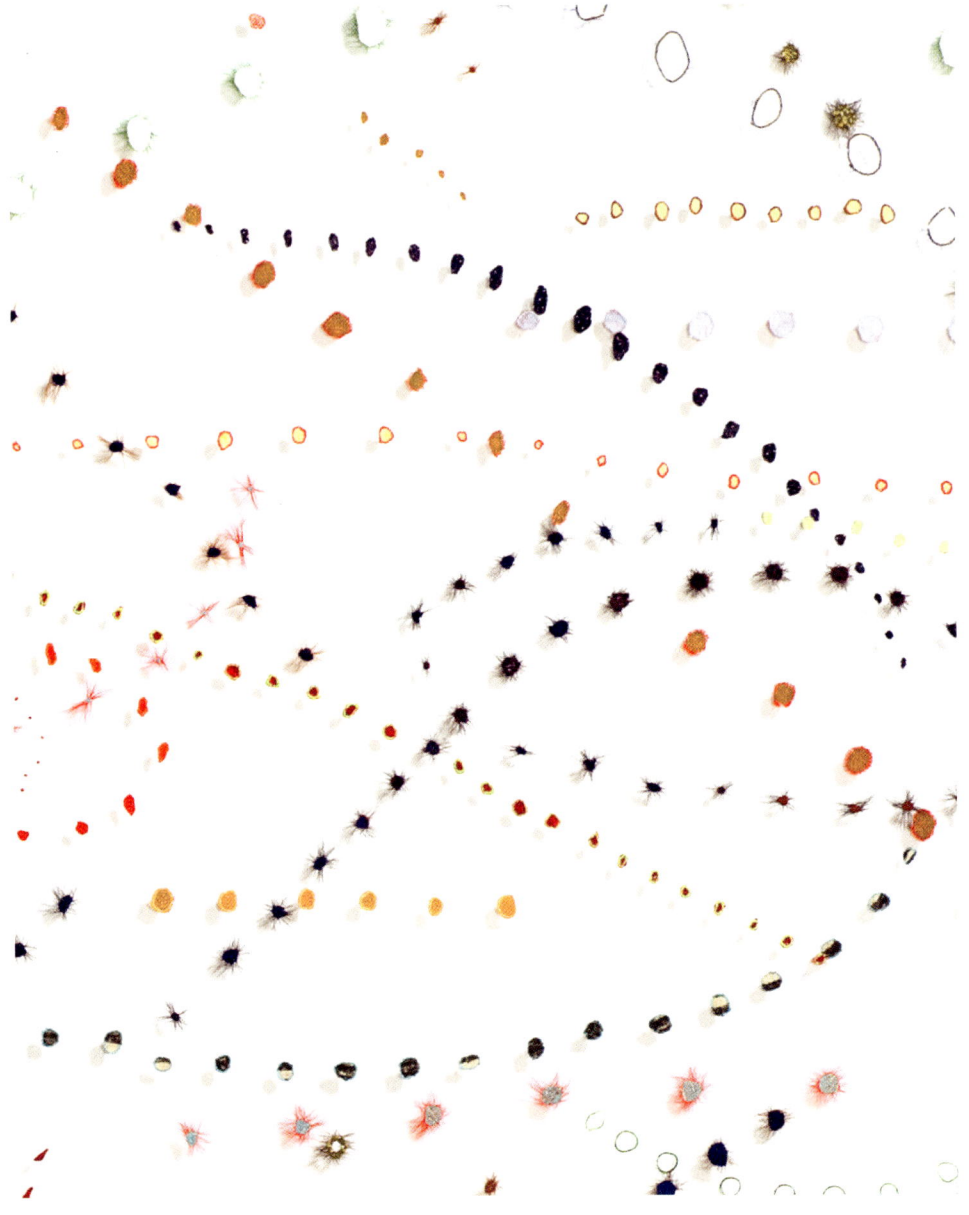

With a dot-dash code of spots, lines and shadows, **Marian Bijlenga** produces works of remarkable delicacy and strength. A meld of opposites is intrinsic to her materials: horsehair, thread, monofilament and fish scales; the finest of materials worked on a monumental scale. When the work floats in front of a wall, shadows double the visual impact.

Her photographs attest to a love of pattern: a trail of insects crawling up a wall in Mali, cracks in the desert earth, or leaf veins found in her garden. Bijlenga mines the patterns of nature, culture and process. Decorative dot patterns from other cultures inspire three works: *India*, *Japan*, and *Congo*, all transformed by connecting fish scales with monofilament.

'Palimpsest' means working over an erased surface. Bijlenga began the *Palimpsest* series in honor of her colleague Herman Scholte, who constructed irregularly shaped weavings directly on the wall. After she painstakingly transferred thirty years of his pin marks to her own studio wall, she covered each pinhole with a unique dot of color, connecting it to the next with an invisible thread.

Her studio is in a former hospital in Amsterdam and her collections of natural objects are arranged to graphic perfection on two walls. Her working wall is also full of pinholes — the marks of process. Like floating calligraphy, *Shadow Dots* results from patterns found in tracings of her own years of pinning and unpinning. Pattern, process and precision mark Bijlenga's art.

detail: *Palimpsest 1*, 2007, overall dimensions 106 x 108", opposite left: *Shadow Dots,* 2010, dimensions variable, right, detail: *Shadow Dots*

Courtesy of the artist and Cervini Haas Fine Art, Scottsdale, AZ

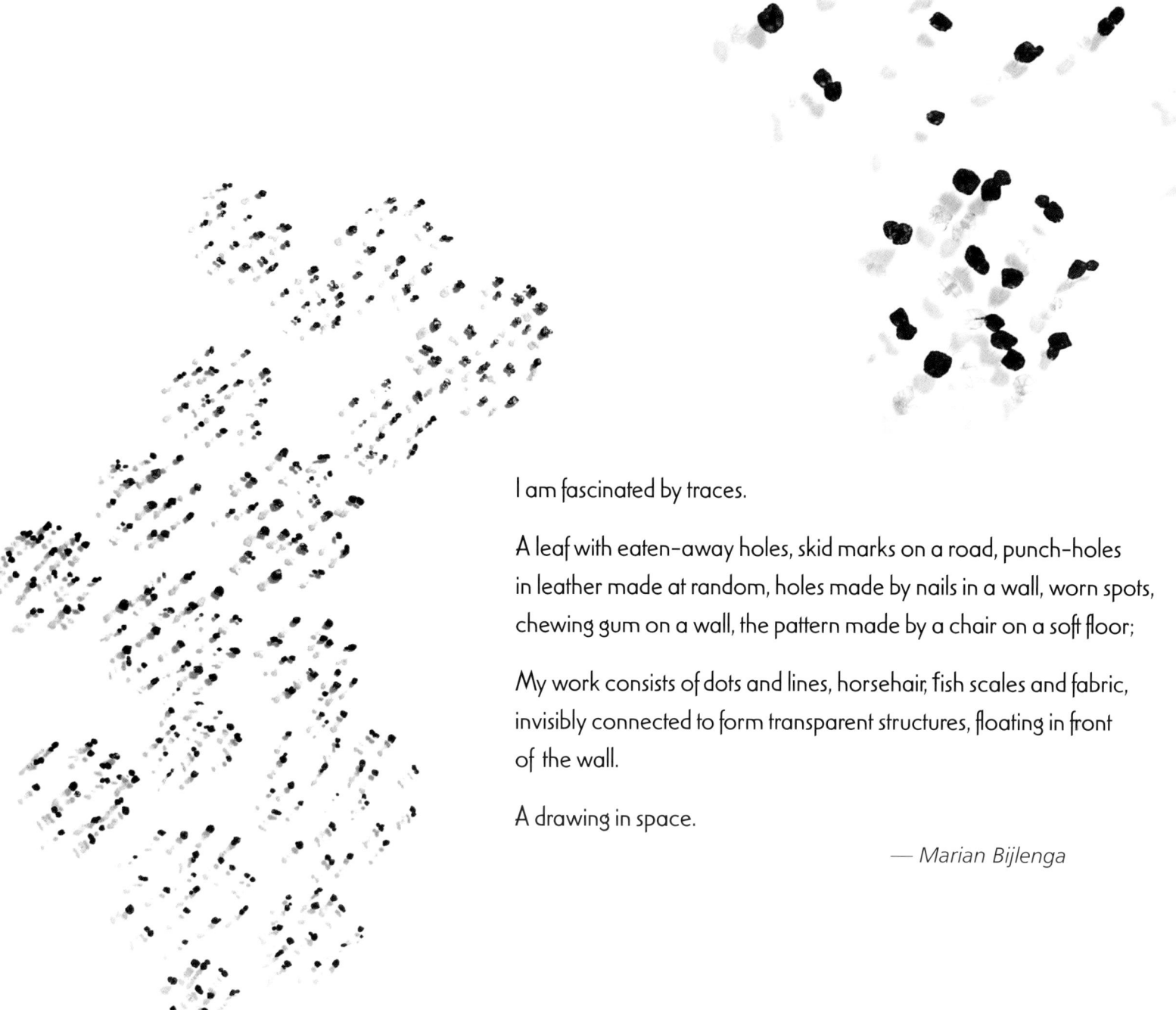

I am fascinated by traces.

A leaf with eaten-away holes, skid marks on a road, punch-holes
in leather made at random, holes made by nails in a wall, worn spots,
chewing gum on a wall, the pattern made by a chair on a soft floor;

My work consists of dots and lines, horsehair, fish scales and fabric,
invisibly connected to form transparent structures, floating in front
of the wall.

A drawing in space.

— *Marian Bijlenga*

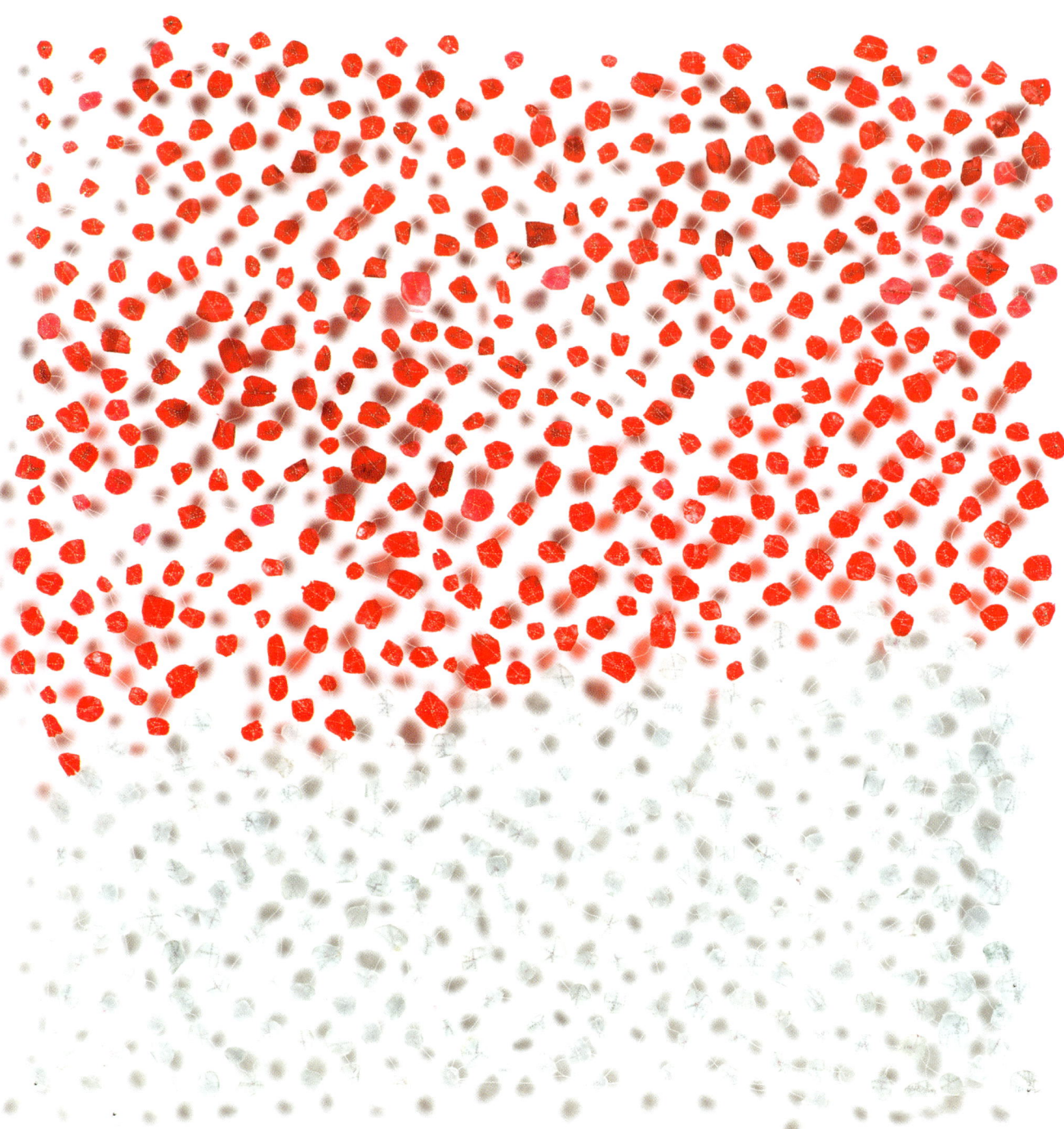

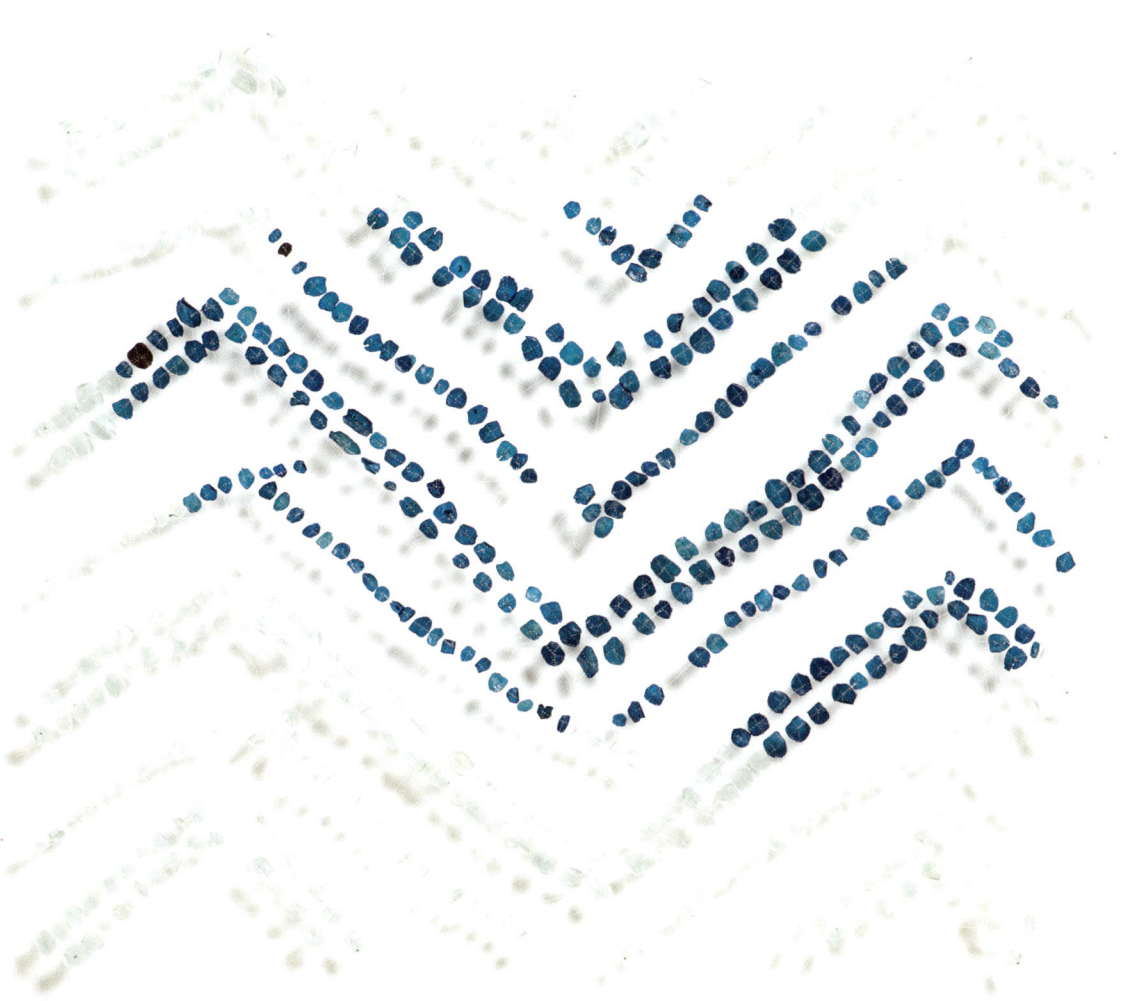

left: *Japan*, 2010, 23.5 x 23.5", right: *India*, 2010, 23.5 x 23.5", below: detail, *India*

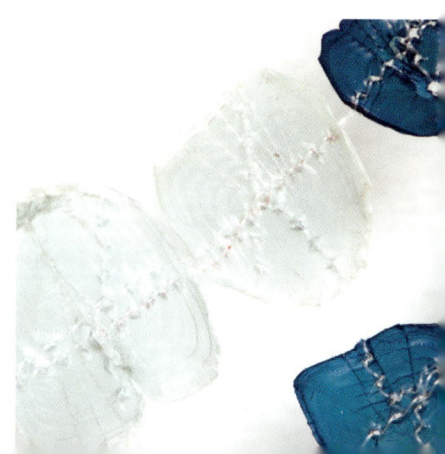

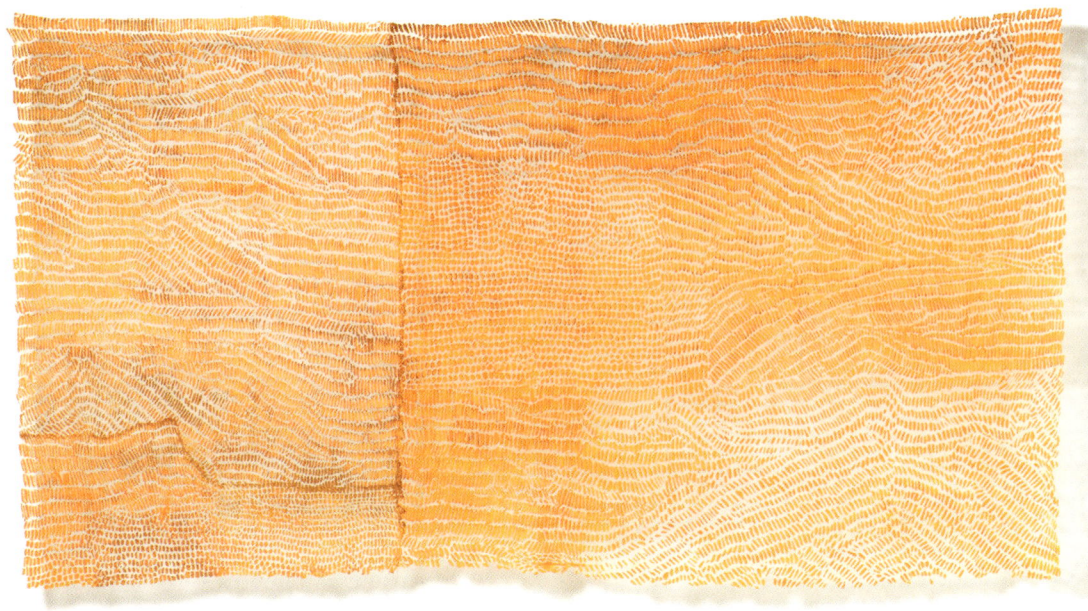

a remnant: Helianthus, 2010, 48 x 84", detail below. *Soulskin: Seeding the Prairie*

Susan Lordi Marker describes this experience: "Walking through nine-foot-tall prairie grass, I turn a corner and suddenly am surrounded by masses of fireflies hovering over masses of tiny yellow sunflowers. All fragile moving parts making patterns and repetitions, encircling me, and resonating collectively in a low hum. Very surprising, as I know they were not there the day before!"

In the natural world of abundance, a rhythmic patterning appears to her; a visual control on all that seems chaotic. This inspires her studio work, "imposing my own ordering of marks on cloth." Transforming a large whole cloth with numberless marks conveys this overwhelming sense to the viewer.

Technically her methods parallel that of building and rebuilding the prairie. She digs into the cloth as well as adding to the surface using a variety of processes, including dévoré, a burning-out technique that etches into the fabric, and cloqué, a method of manipulating fibers with lye that simultaneously shrinks and prods the fabric up and above the flat cloth surface. Stitching, etching and shrinking result in a permanent restructuring of the cloth, changing both its shape and the way it hangs in space. Like seeing what is revealed as the winter snows melt each year on the prairie, the cloth responds in its own unpredictable way. Marker welcomes this new final form.

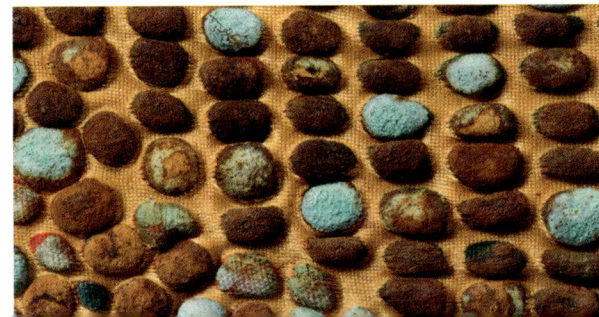

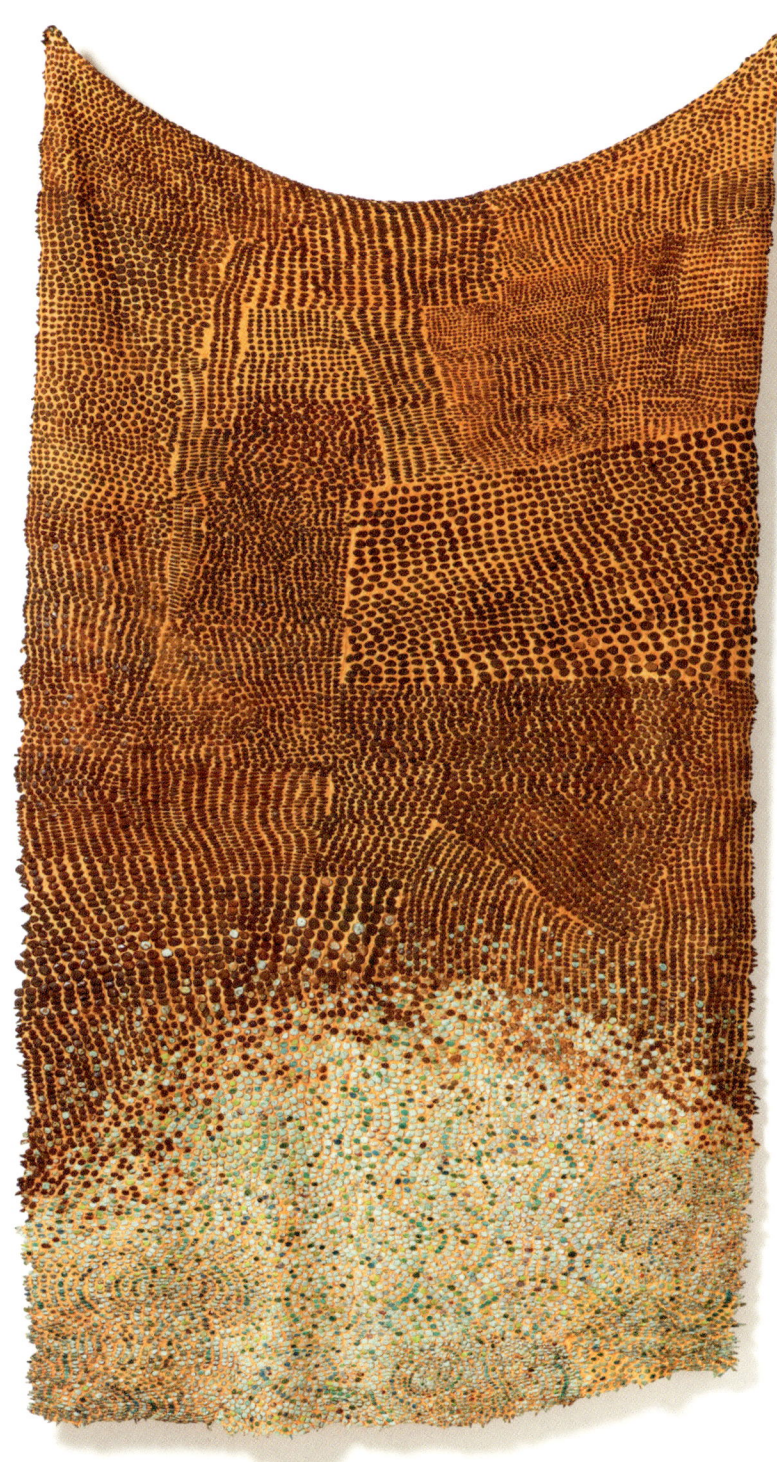

For several years I have been restoring a small native tallgrass prairie. My work reflects my fascination with the overwhelming number of elements that surround me when I am immersed in this natural environment. I work in response to nature's rhythm. I am conscious of thousands of elements being coded — fitting together — and it is this orchestration that inspires me. A harmony of flight patterns over the water; a cacophony of calls and cries at dawn; a simple repetitive drumbeat of an incessant insect record both auditory and visual patterns, movement, or rhythm. I am interested in their collective effect, and I want the whole cloth I make to suggest that same experience for the viewer when they first encounter my work.

— *Susan Lordi Marker*

Soulskin: Seeding the Prairie, 2000, 80 x 42"

Time inhabits **Nancy Erickson's** work. Humans and animals move through ancient domains adorned by cave drawings and ceremonial markings. Though her focus is on the past, they can be read as allegories for a post-apocalyptic world. She worked within a rectangular format until a decade ago, then 'freed' her characters from the frame to move about the wall. Freedom added a new tension to the work, involving the viewer with the compositional space. The pattern of lines and drawings on each figure is noteworthy, suggesting tattoos, piercing; marks to protect and marks to camouflage; traces of time.

Her works in *Traces* evoke three aspects of Erickson's message. Both *Vigilance* and *Caldera* are gripping in their sense of imminent danger and keeping watch; the destructive power of nature and man. The lyrical *Miracle of a Spring Shower* poses its green woman enjoying the luxury of a passing cloud.

Together captures her desire for human and animal mutual regard and respect. Erickson, who lives up a steep canyon in Montana, bemoans her naïve 'back to nature' neighbors who move up the canyon to 'get away from it all' and later discover bears raiding their garbage.

The high key palette she employs underscores her message, lobbying visually on the side of nature, human and wild. Not only is ancient time a force in her work, but so is a call to the present: There may not be much time left.

The Miracle of a Spring Shower, 2007, 71 x 41", right: detail, *The Miracle of a Spring Shower*
right: *Caldera*, 2010, 74 x 64"

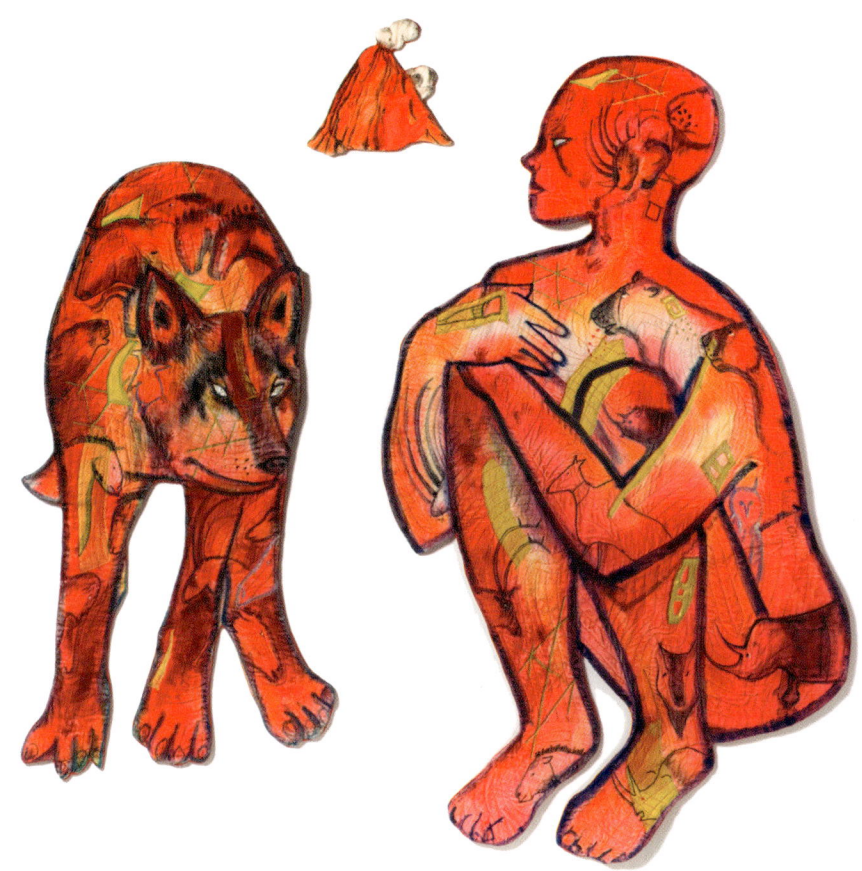

Traces fits well with what I have been making for many years. Paraphrased here, a trace is a mark or line left by anything that has passed: a trail, a sign or evidence of some past thing; something drawn; a barely discernible quantity, quality or characteristic. Something to track down. Each of these meanings is evident to me in the creation of these works.

— *Nancy Erickson*

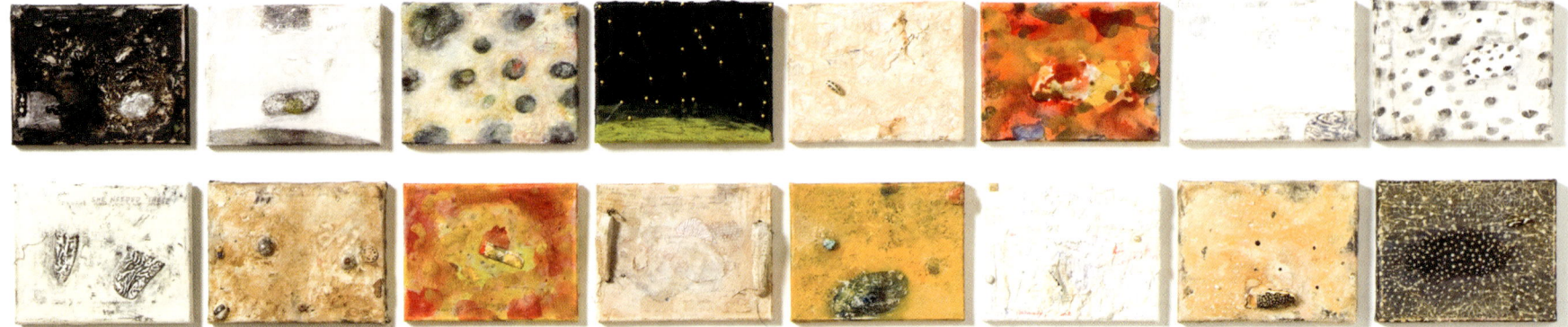

Connecting idea and object compels **Carol Ann Carter**. "Tracking visual thinking … literally and metaphorically … connections … figure to its environment, needles to fiber, travel between cultures … healing and repair; the intersections of art and life."

Intellectual engagement and the sheer physicality of her work command attention. About *Solo Moments* Carter writes, "I've addressed the notion of the floating self and traced imagined or constructed characters' behavior in several environments." Superimposed and embedded objects, strong contrasts of light and dark; mysterious markings draw us in and allow our imaginations full play.

From heavily textured and sculptural work, she freely crosses the boundaries of media, pursuing her initial idea into digital drawings that in turn are transformed into videos, partnering with Joshua Toney Kendall. Luminous layers — sound and movement — enhance the floating self in *Flying Solos*. We are suspended over a world of multi-dimensions, suggesting a tidal reef or the inner workings of the mind.

Back on Earth, *Body Objeckte* alludes to "a degree of pleasure and pain present in the same entity or field." They reveal scars of experience suggesting hurt and healing.

Medicine Boxes, an expressive coda, are "small gestures distilling and compressing the weight of the larger works." Constructed with found and collected objects embedded in or secured to paper mâché, these fetishistic containers project the power of belief, healing and potential resolution that connect to Carter's continuing exploration.

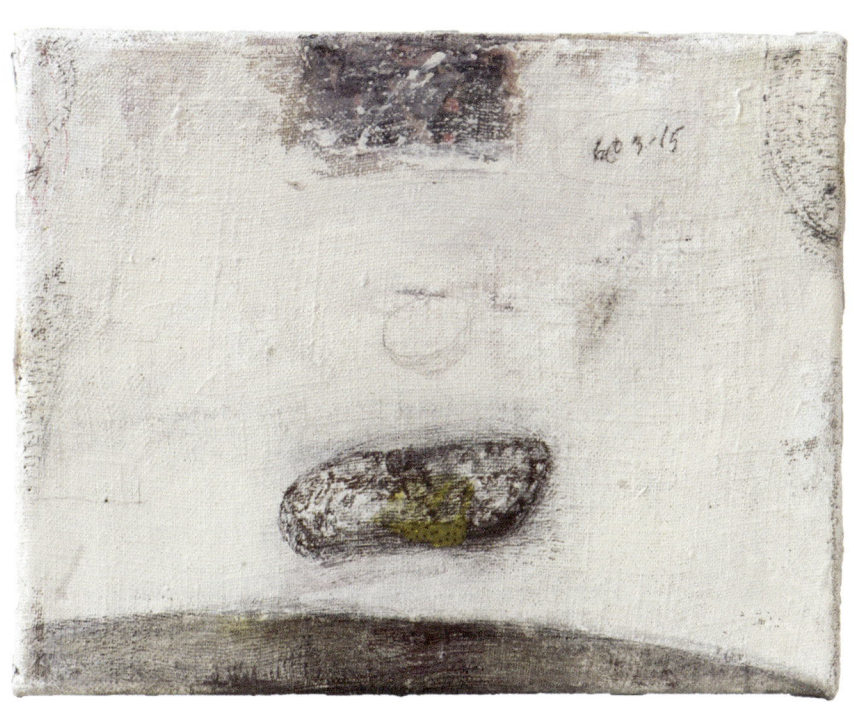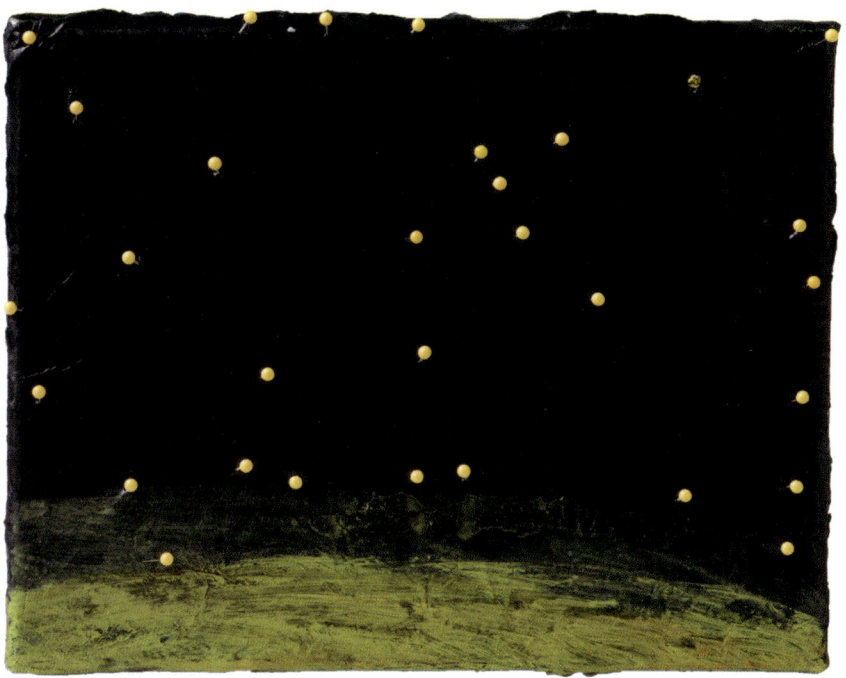

left: *Solo Moments,* 2010, 16 x 80", above details: *Solo Moments*

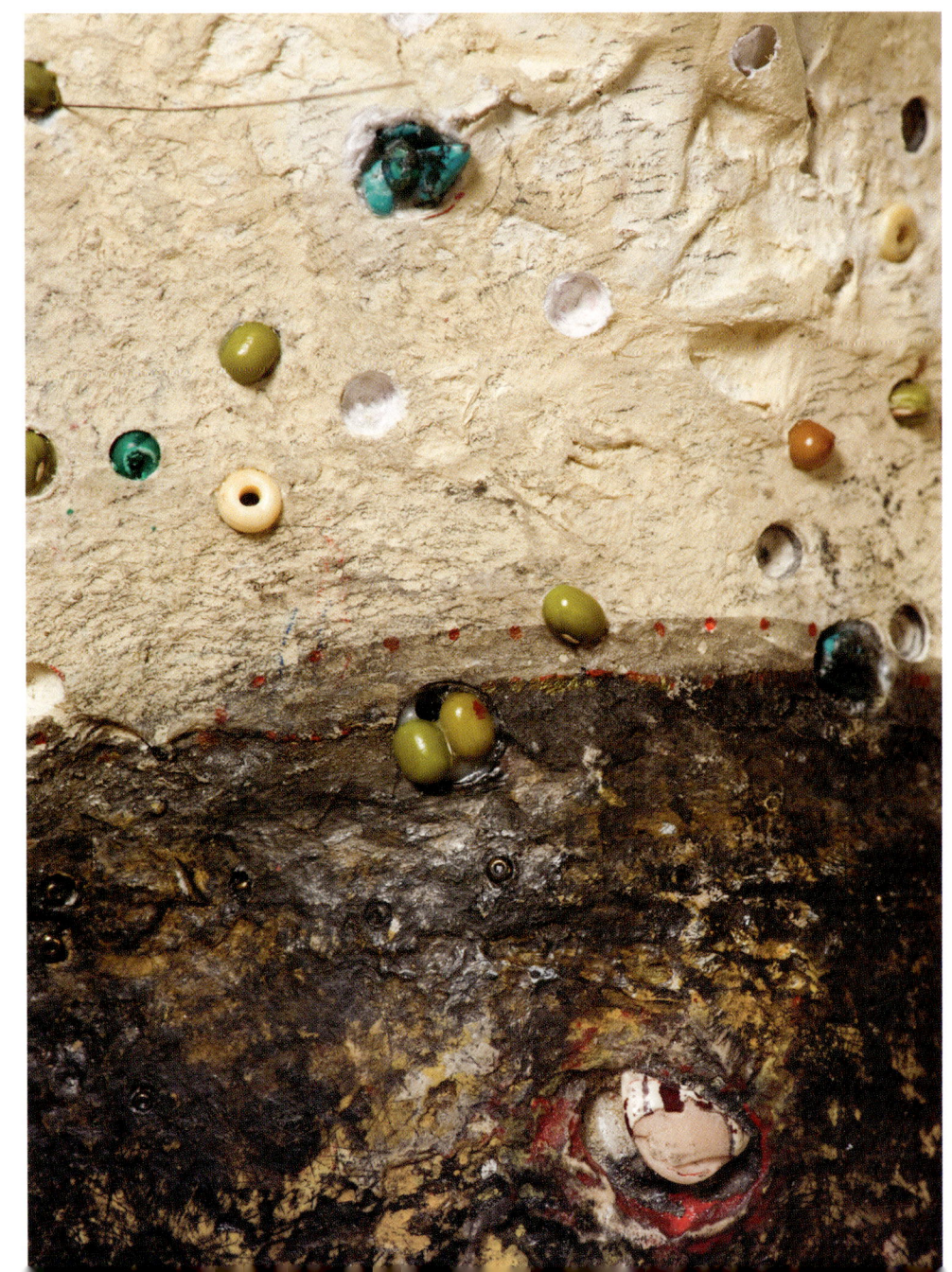

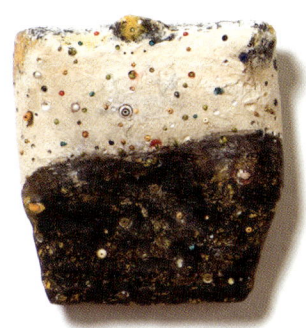 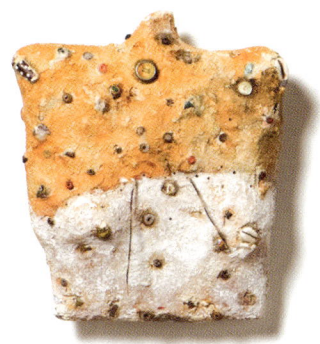 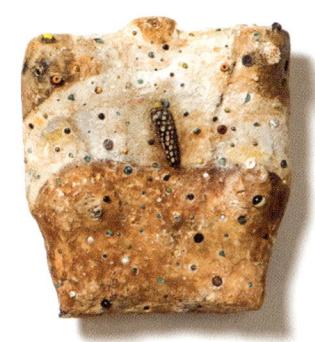 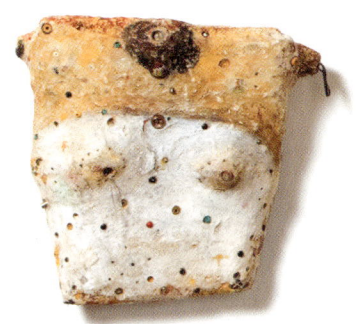 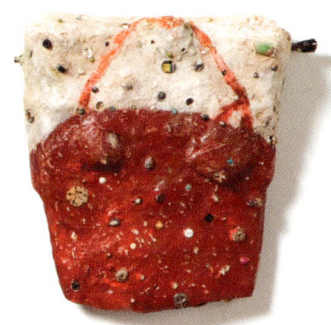

To trace means to discover by following the development of one thing as it leads to another. My 'inter-media' work involves constructing objects, but also making digital drawings, creating installations and video. I explore the connections or relationships among things: memories to narratives, mediums, generations and ultimately, art to life. My own mixed ethnicity — primarily African and traces that include European and Native American — as well as coming of age in the 60s and 70s, and my travels since, have influenced my creative directions.

I wish to thank my assistants Kelsey Yankey and Ashley Flinn for their wisdom and dedicated help in constructing these works.

— *Carol Ann Carter*

detail left: *Body Objeckte*, above: *Body Objeckte*, 2008-2010, 12 x 11 x 3" each

Dorothy Caldwell listens to the sound of silent spaces. Silence allows an Australian aborigine to listen to a song of direction, an internal map. Caldwell comments, "As well as giving direction, it is telling the history and mythology written on the land. This might be accompanied by a visual component — a series of colorful dots that to us are amazing contemporary paintings, but for those who understand the language, they are maps." The maps sing the lay of the land. In the Arctic a young Inuit learns his way around the land, recording and remembering every aspect. Now he may use GPS assistance, but if the batteries fail, he still knows where he is.

A year of travel marks Caldwell's research in the Australian Outback and the Canadian Arctic, areas where indigenous people are "rooted in their relationships with their landscapes." *Fjord* and *How Do We Know When It's Night?* are the first two works this research inspired. Monumental in scale, they consume our peripheral vision and stretch far.

Caldwell assigns her territory personal markings. She scribes patterns from *A Book of Marks*. Inspired by the "beauty of stripes and checks" in a Japanese kimono sample book, Caldwell made her own book of drawn and painted marks. She enlarged patterns and silkscreened them, using resist techniques combined with direct calligraphic marks on the powerful new works. As we learn Caldwell's mapping vocabulary, we 'sing' our way through her landscape.

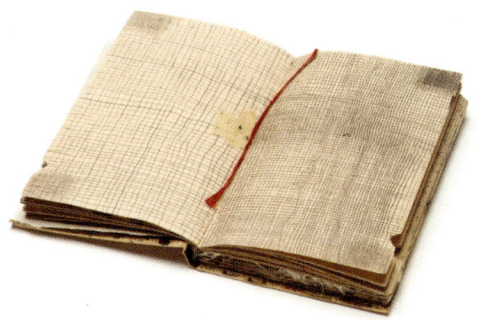

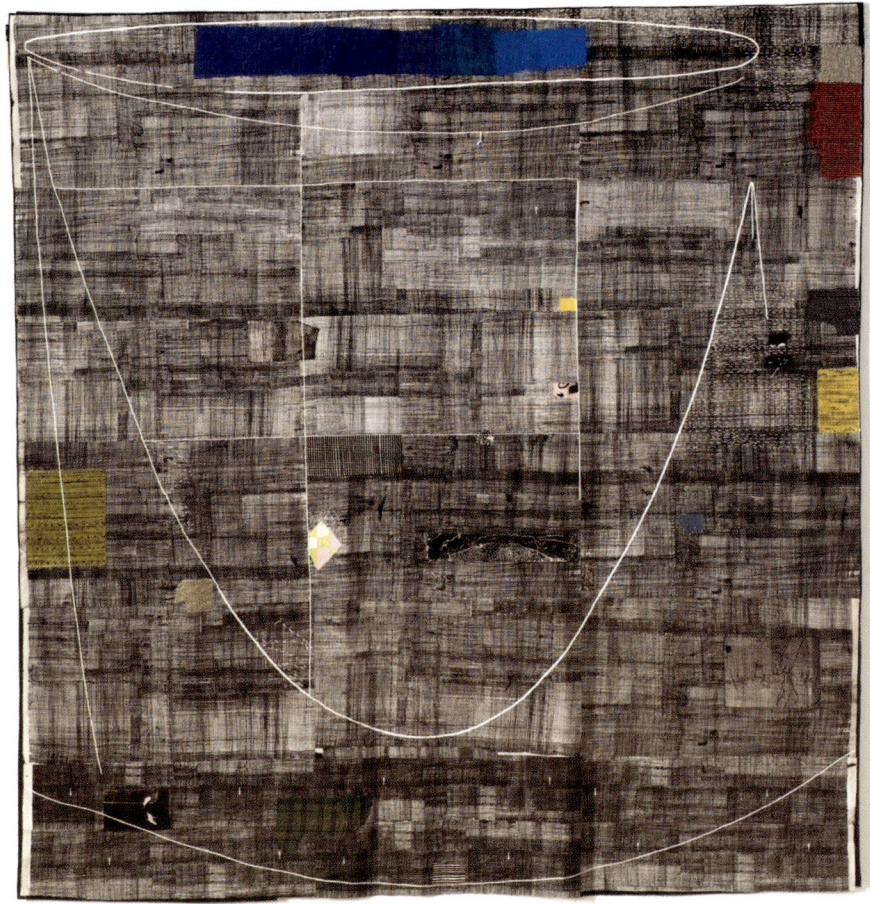

Fjord, 2010, 120 x 114", below left: *Book of Marks,* 2007-2008, 8.5 x 14" open

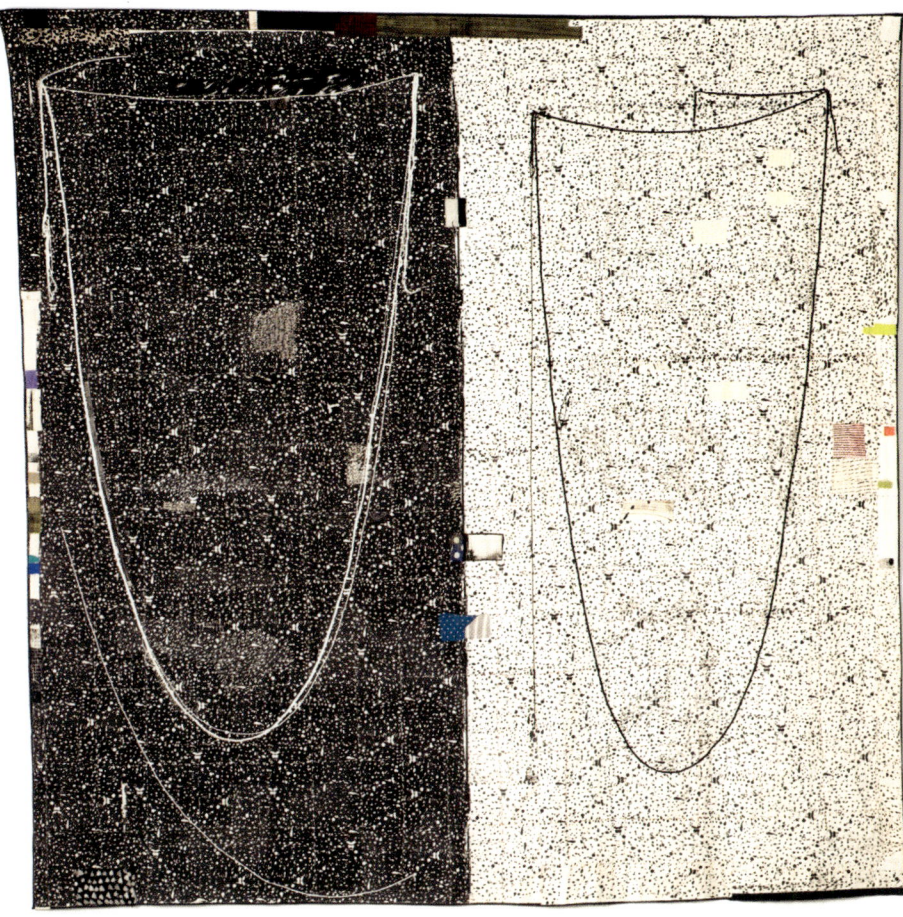

How Do We Know When It's Night?, 2010 , 120 x 114"
detail right: *How Do We Know When It's Night?*

My work is an ongoing investigation of the meaning of place. I investigate how humans mark and shape the land and how these human marks interact with the natural geology. I am intrigued by maps and by organization of land through patterns of settlement and agriculture. I have come to see the dichotomy between conventional mapping and my personal mapping that identifies intimate landmarks and simplifies them into abstract shapes and textures. Maps give a viewpoint of the land filtered through what is important to the mapmaker. I am mapping unfamiliar territory, identifying my personal landmarks through gathering, touching and recording the contents of the landscape. In this way I form a sense of place for myself.

— *Dorothy Caldwell*

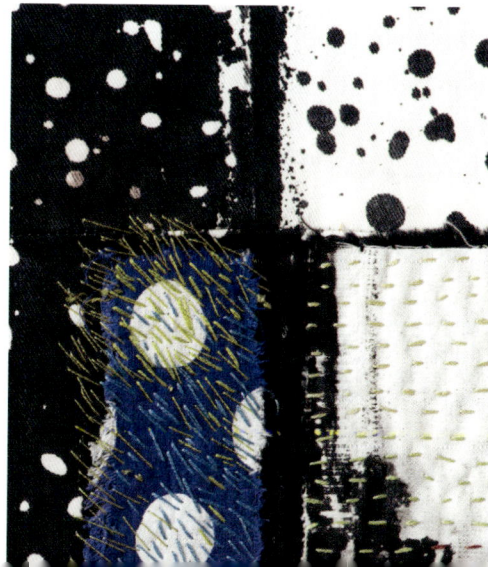

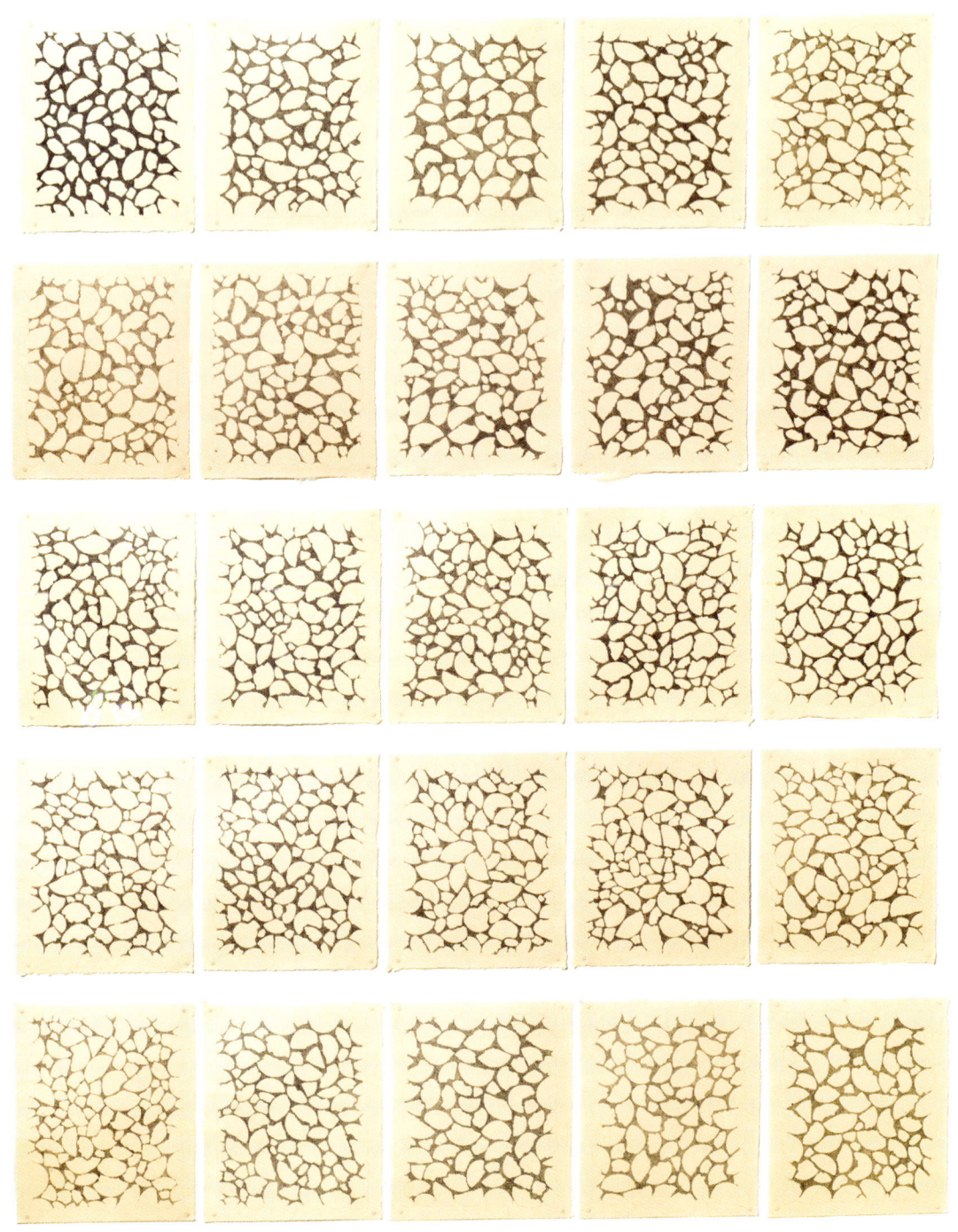

above: *September Diary*, 2002, 132 x 89", right: detail, *September Diary*, below: *Too Late in Asking: A Litany of Loss,* 2010, 16.25 x 38.5" open

On September 11, 2001, **Lou Cabeen** was stunned by the number of dead. She needed to see what "over 3000" looked like, and began to draw. Tracing around broken bits of sand dollars "falling through space," she counted each void to commemorate the broken. This became a daily meditation, resulting in 30 sheets of paper, a *September Diary*. Begun in 2001, this work marks the early edge of the decade covered in *Traces*.

An elegiac tone pervades much of Cabeen's art. *Too Late in Asking: A Litany of Loss*[1] memorializes the land, documenting hundreds of destroyed mountaintops. Cabeen recalls John Prine's *Paradise*: "Well, they dug for their coal till the land was forsaken. Then they wrote it all down as the progress of man." She writes, "I am too late in asking about the health of these mountains, valleys, creeks and communities."

Hope balances despair. Three watersheds that supply her hometown of Seattle are part of the *Geography of Hope* series. The watershed, an area of land that separates waters flowing to other bodies of water, is presented like a strip map stitched on silk organza. The materials suggest fragility and resemble charts of blood flow or brain activity. The wrinkled surface, like aging skin, reminds us of the vulnerability of natural systems. Torn edges imply that this is part of a whole interconnecting global system. Cabeen uses the geographical meaning of watershed here, but *September Diary* documents its other meaning: a turning point.

[1] Number 2 of an edition of 3

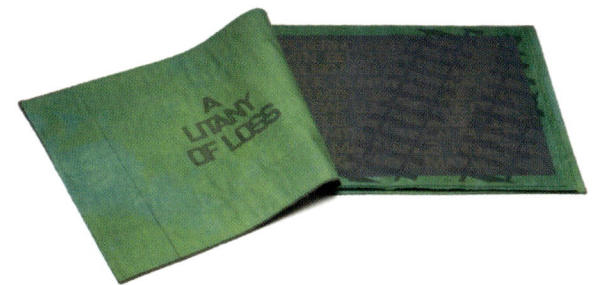

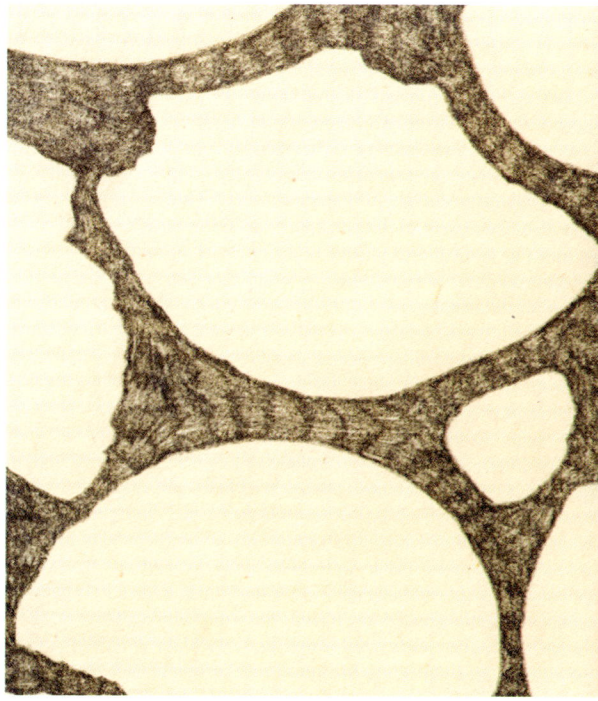

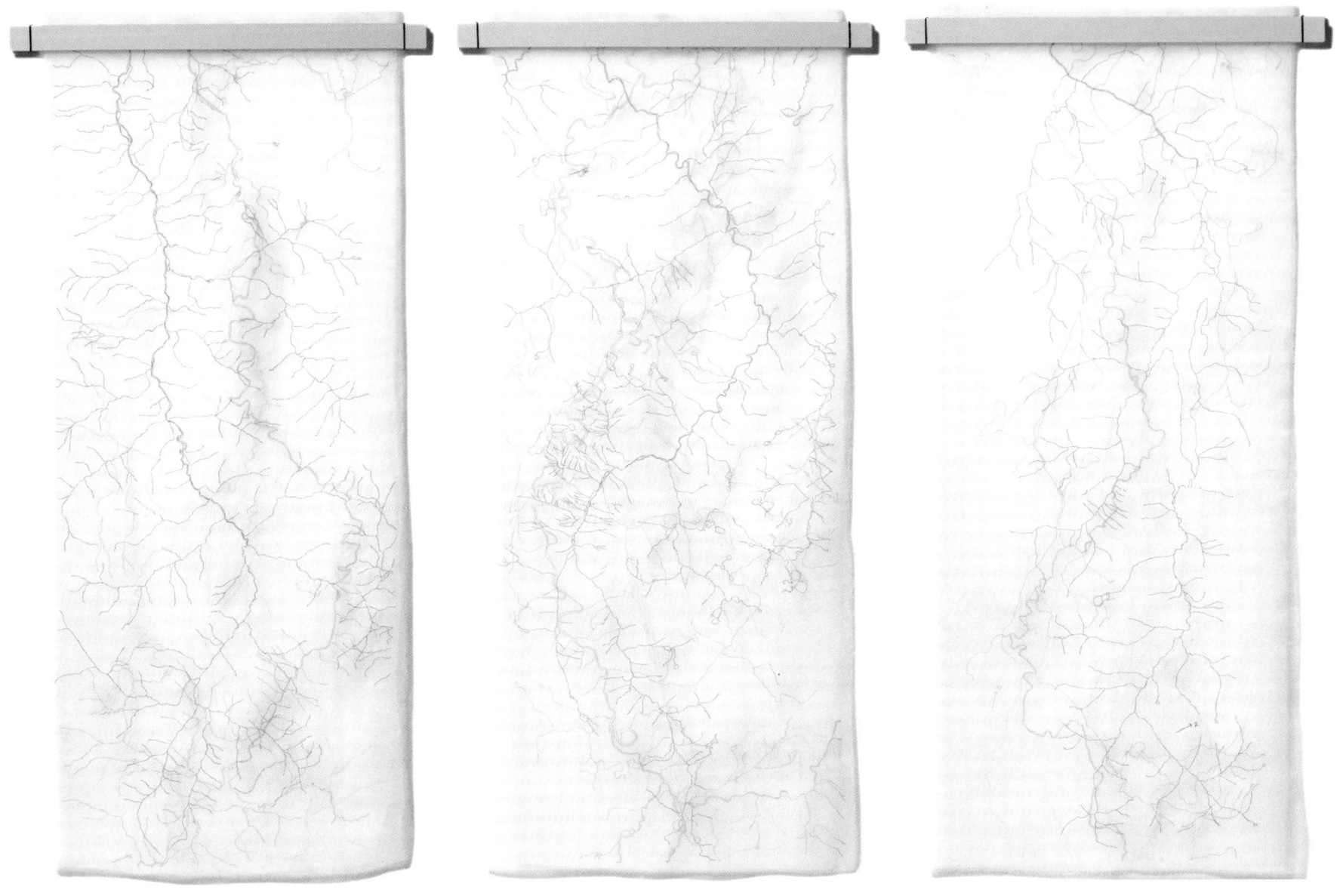

Watershed series: *White River, Snohomish River South, Cedar River,* 2010, 3 works, each 60 x 24", detail opposite: *Watershed: Cedar River*

My work focuses on the Seattle watersheds which are a major feature in my *Geography of Hope* series. The Cedar River Watershed has been protected by the city of Seattle since the 19th century, making our drinking water supply among the safest in the nation. I am witness to the restoration of the Green River Watershed, and appreciate the extraordinary complexity and beauty of the southern portion of the Snohomish River Watershed.

In contrast to this work, I have begun a series titled *Lamentation* with a book titled *Too Late in Asking: A Litany of Loss*. The book offers names of hundreds of mountains lost to mountaintop removal mining in Appalachia. These mountaintops and their valley streams form the headwaters of watersheds through central Appalachia that are now seriously compromised. Although I live and work far from these damaged systems, I know that ultimately we all live downstream.

Thanks to studio assistants Hannah Riker and Hannah Levi.

— *Lou Cabeen*

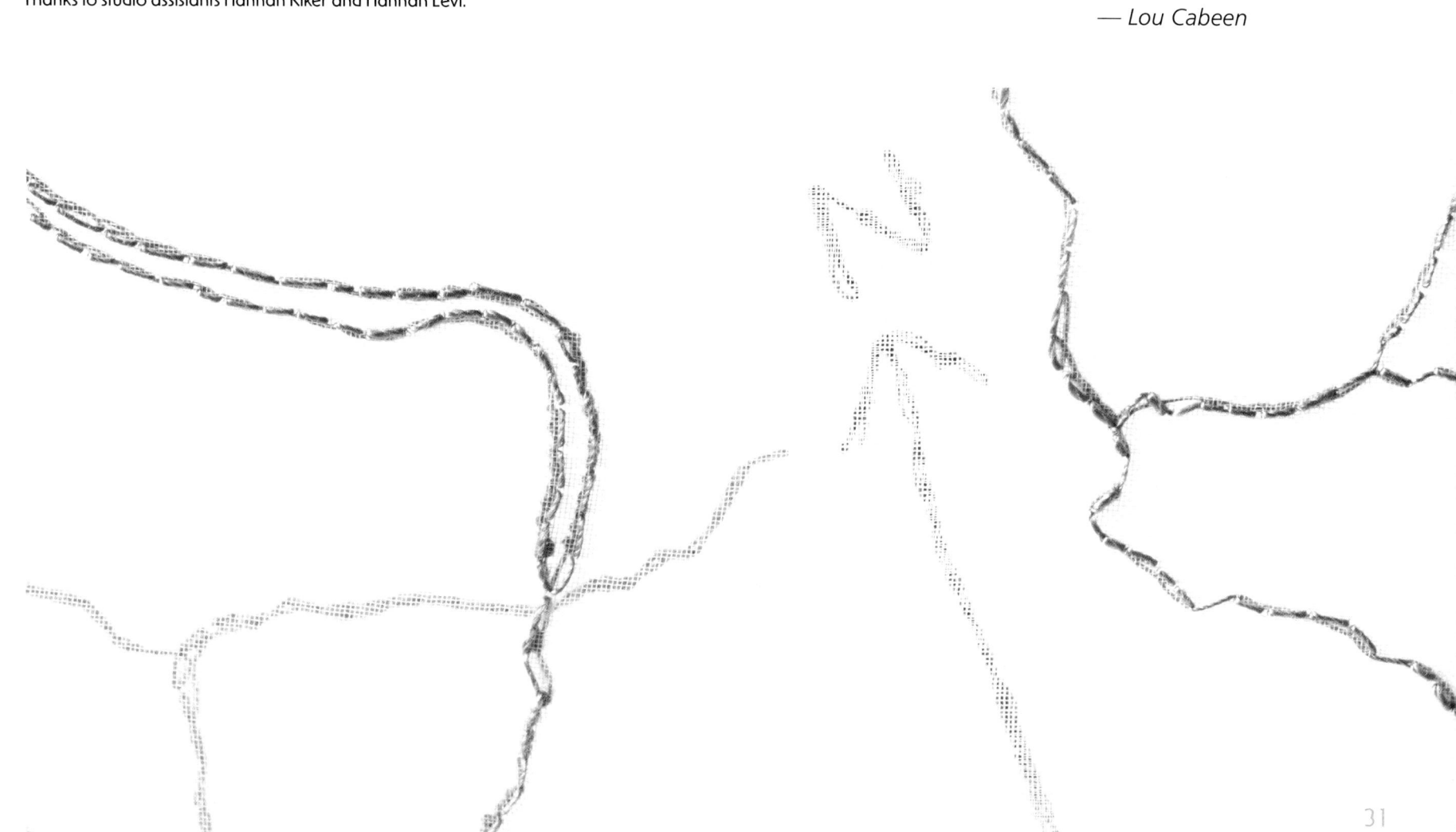

Gail Rieke assembles moments of the unexpected in her journals and distills a "sense of awe into some core configuration that transmits the impact of the moment." One of her assembled travel journals, *Blaze of Glory/Japan and Korea 2007-2009* reflects three journeys to Japan and Korea. Each experience created "a visual journey of the imagination that parallels the actual experience." *Blaze of Glory* is meant to be interactive, but we experience it vicariously, imagining examining the layers of boxes, books, pamphlets and pouches that comprise the whole. Notebooks documenting a day of experience; found and formed objects; old, patched fabrics and new, her assemblages form and reform time evoking the artistic observer's spirit.

Rieke tracks the circular aspect of time in *Summer Fall Winter Spring*.[1] This calendar in the round examines time as cyclical rather than linear. On a base of semi-transparent Mylar wedge-like segments, each drawing overlays the previous one, not totally obscuring what came before, but forming a new, more complex image, like a tracery of buried treasure. For Rieke, this is "a visual mirroring of the way memory feels to me. One can always excavate down through the layers and see clearly something that has been buried in time as one might do by looking at a photograph or hearing a particular song."

[1] Container for this work made by Sialia Rieke.

"Ichigo ichie" is a Japanese phrase which can be literally translated to mean "one moment — one meeting." A longer definition is: "This moment is singular; it will never come again; Be completely present in this moment." I delight in the paradox of being completely immersed in this moment while simultaneously responding to the experience in some creative way that will capture the moment in time, and preserve it in an historical artistic context. The sensibility of awareness and gratitude for even the simplest of things — a real humility — this is what I would like to learn in the inextricably united process of my life-work and artwork.

— *Gail Rieke*

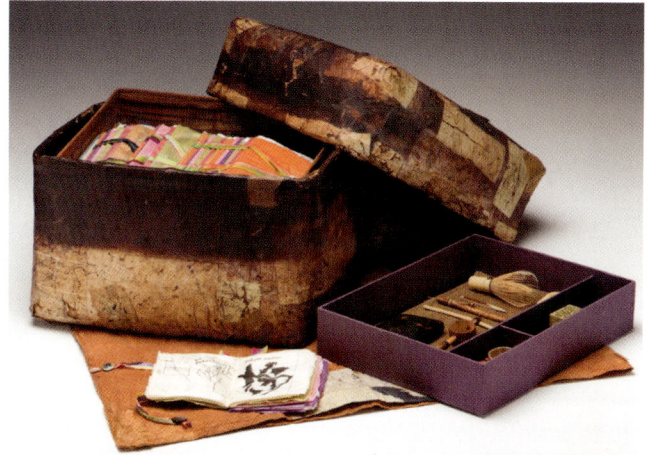

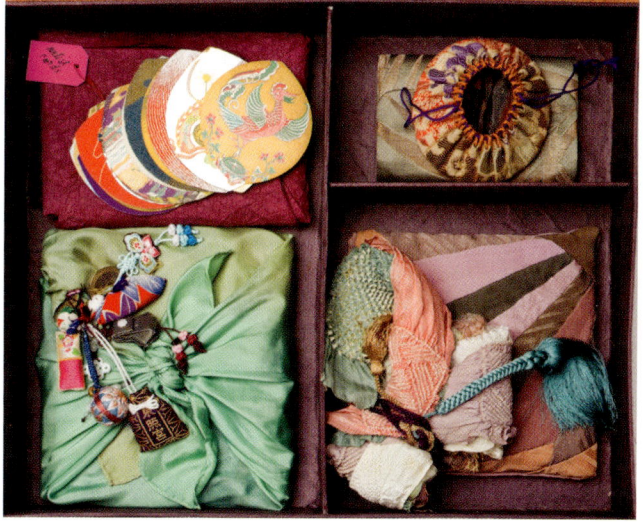

left: *Summer Fall Winter Spring*, 2008, 38" diameter, right: *Blaze of Glory/Japan and Korea 2007-2009*, dimensions variable

Marc Dombrosky, a poet of the streets, installs urban detritus — lists, photos, fragments of envelopes — obsessively overstitched, thereby recasting the daily flotsam of life into a conversation about partial memory, loss and separation. He finds these relics of life lived wherever he journeys. "When we moved to Las Vegas, we moved into an environment experiencing one of the most violent economic disasters of modern times, yet continues to build." *His mouth and eyes expressed the double* reflect this mix of futility and heightened energy.

For Dombrosky, the vitrines in which the work is installed are part of the work, not just protecting, but also sharing the history of the works they temporarily housed in prior museum exhibitions. The museum is a 'safe house' providing protection except, perhaps, from a critical glare.

Dombrosky's stitched bits of life poignantly evoke those who lost or tossed lists and love letters, photographs or check stubs. Slow progress and easy failure reverberate through his collection of discards. His is a street that is easy to overlook on the way to Somewhere Else.

Embroidery mends some of the sadness. "Embroidery places its own heavy (historical and physical) content onto the pieces … A love letter that's been embroidered by hand means something different than a love letter scrawled in pencil, but maybe one is more flawed, maybe not." No easy answers here, but a reflection on gaps, the spaces of memory and human connection.

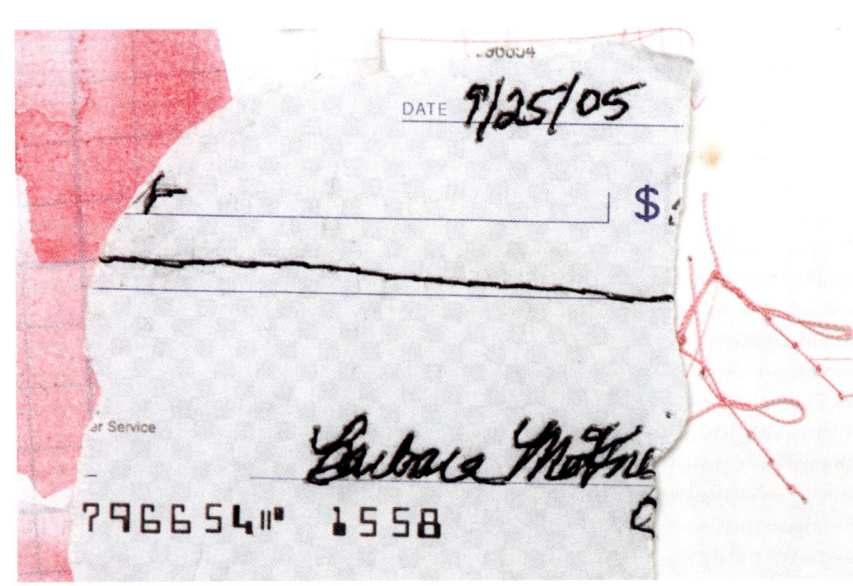

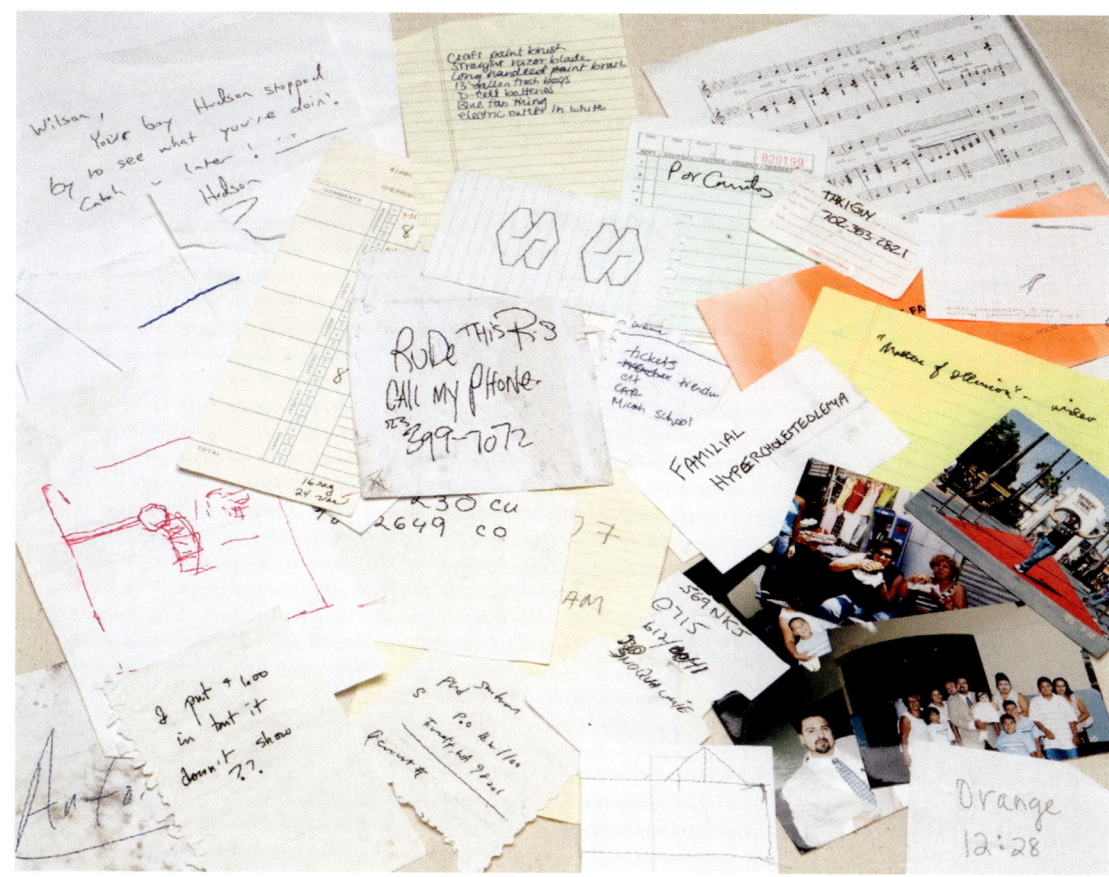

His mouth and eyes expressed the double (part 2), 2010, dimensions variable, left, detail: *His mouth and eyes expressed the double (part 1)*, 2010, dimensions variable

Courtesy of the artist and Platform Gallery, Seattle, WA

The title of my artwork, *His mouth and eyes expressed the double* comes from a phrase in Apollinaire's short story, "The Poet Assassinated." It describes the protagonist moving quickly through the streets of Paris, navigating both his immediate surroundings and his memory simultaneously. The work presents a fragmentary conversation — or a conversation of fragments — that allows a viewer/reader a position within the work. Any one of us could have picked up or written these scraps, torn this envelope open or lost this photograph. By shipping them from across the country and bringing them together in Raleigh, the work is built around the sense of a deep separation or removal from the original space of writing and loss, both psychologically and physically. The trace becomes an opportunity to observe, pretend, intone, suggest, and disavow what may have happened somewhere.

— *Marc Dombrosky*

Dichotomies prevail in **Clare Verstegen's** work. She explores the tension exhibited in the moment of stasis; a balance that may tip at any moment.

To further emphasize the contradictory elements that fascinate her, she uses unlikely combinations of materials and techniques that lay claim to a balancing act all their own. Silkscreen printing, the epitome of changing a surface, is applied to an unlikely ground — dense wool felt. The layered images are absorbed, softened and modified by the deeply textured felt. Further markings with wood-burning tools add relief texture and alter the colors. The frame containing the soft felt provides a contrasting hard element, and projects it out from the wall.

Our minds play with shifting images that look controlled, but have the promise of chaos. Natural elements coexist with measuring devices, games of chance, and arrays of numbers. In the past, Verstegen has pictured a life preserver, but it has been replaced by rows of Cheerios in her visual vocabulary. Cheerios juxtaposed with dice are a chancy combination of healthy eating and risky behavior. Will we need the safety pins that seem to hold the work together?

Verstegen's small 'sermons in stones' attract with rich and inviting colors and strong graphics. They are like spending time with a teacher who speaks in parables from which we learn to appreciate the wonder of opposing elements of our lives.

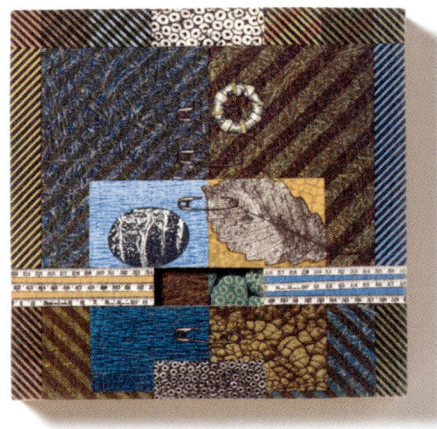 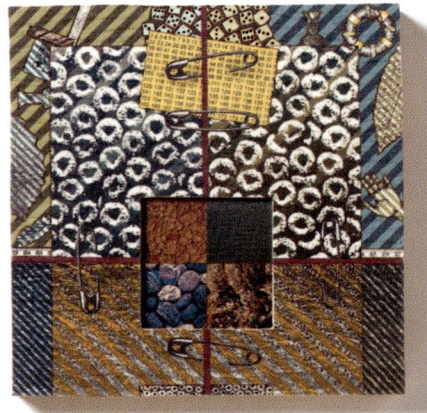 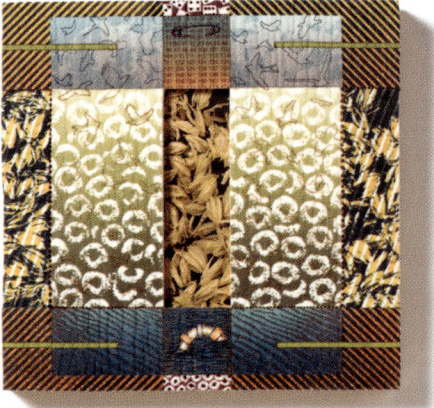

Safety Measures (left), 2009, *Reminders* (middle), 2010, *Tracing* (right), 2010, 18 x 18 x 1.75" each
right: *Transition* (lt. top), 2010, *Ascent* (mid. top), 2010, *Between* (rt. top), 2010, *Shifting* (lt. bottom), 2010, *Passage* (mid. bottom), 2010, *Water Level* (rt. bottom), 2008, 10 x 10 x 2.5" each

The threshold between opposing conditions and the effort to maintain balance is a fundamental issue in the works I create. To be on the brink of contrary circumstances underscores the moment of transition between light and shadow, floating and sinking, pleasure and pain, conscious and unconscious, sound and silence, and life and death. I recognize the shifting patterns, cycles and forces of nature as symbolic and constant reminders of the passing of time and a sense of urgency. Observing, recording, collecting and interpreting traces of the natural world generates various aspects of the visual and metaphorical language I develop. Stones worn smooth, lush grass faded to brown, leaves fallen to decay, and brilliant flowers turned dry and brittle reveal evidence of a past existence.

— *Clare Verstegen*

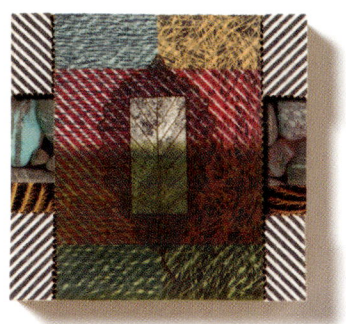
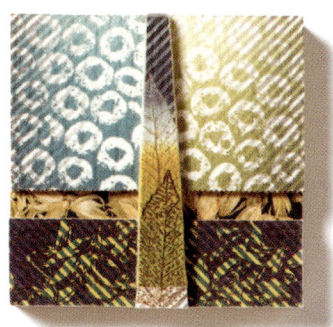
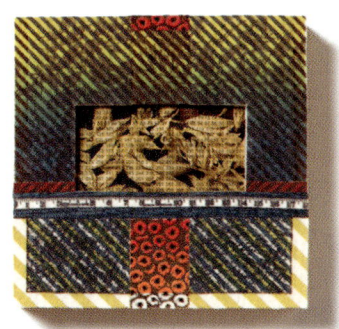
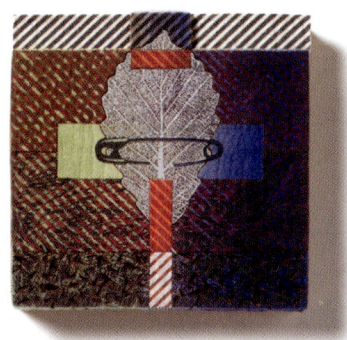
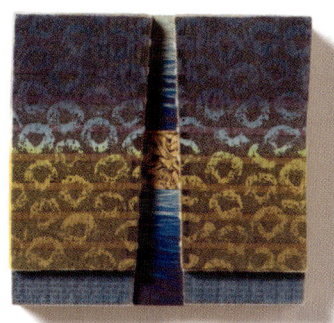
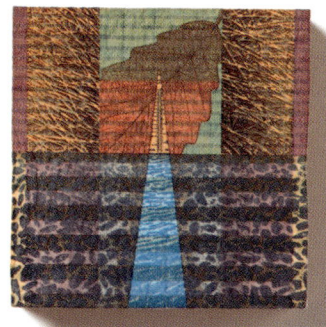

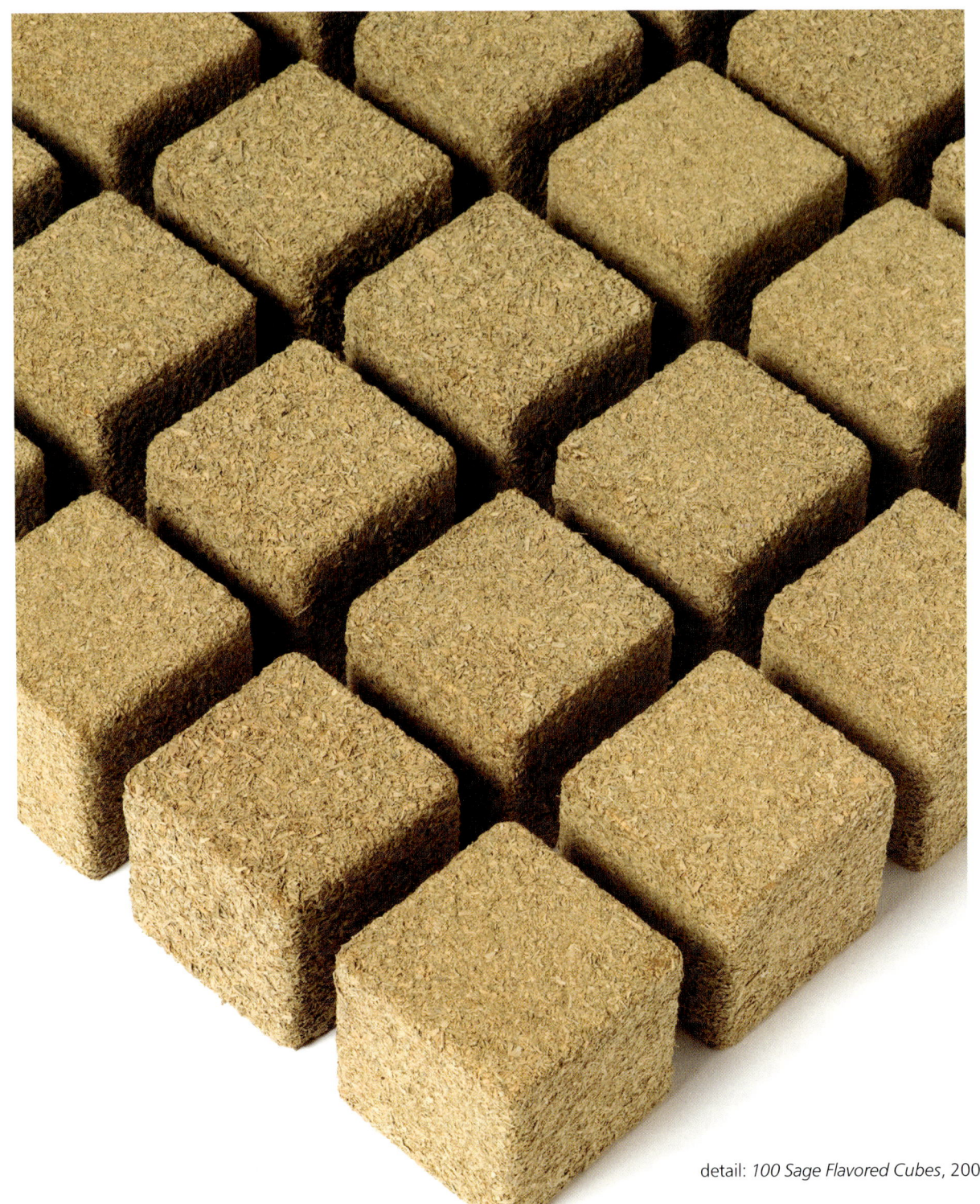

My works are produced as a result of an ongoing conversation with nature. Gathering and collecting objects and materials are essential to my working process. I respectfully approach environmental processing by incorporating recycled natural as well as man-made materials, most of which I have gathered, in my work. From the moment of collecting, I begin a collaboration with these objects and materials. In the process I examine nature and its changes to understand the elements of its language: shape, pattern, color, texture and scale. I need to understand this language to create work that carries the beauty and power that I see and feel in nature.

— *Kyoung Ae Cho*

detail: *100 Sage Flavored Cubes*, 2007, overall dimensions 60 x 60 x 3.5", each cube 3.5 x 3.5 x 3.5"

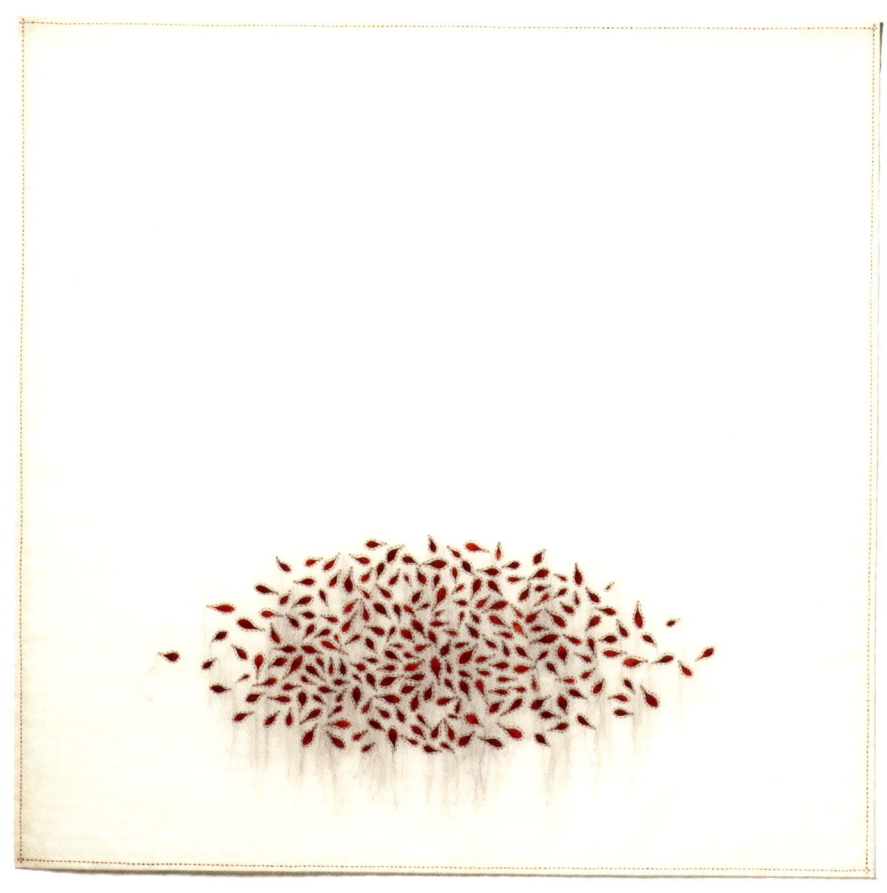

Fallen, 2010, 42 x 42"

Kyoung Ae Cho converses with nature. *100 Sage Flavored Cubes* had its first life as an installation made from wild sage bushes gathered in the arid lands near Walla Walla, Washington, and positioned into a circular mound 20 feet in diameter. Dismantled and stored for almost a decade, the dialogue recommenced as she restructured the dry materials into three and a half inch cubes and its current geometric form.

A city gardener, Cho maintains an open attitude toward plants that arrive of their own free will. Weeds may be welcome, but trees are pulled before they take hold. The seedlings eventually find their way into her work. "While pulling these baby trees with beautiful roots I am thinking of the potential/possibility that these plants could become." *Broken Dream*, made from roots and burn marks on paper, suggest the potential of choice, growth, order and decay.

In *Fallen*, she contemplates plants and people. "We cover our body to protect and to decorate. Plants do that with leaves and flowers. But unlike us, most plants … dress up more when it gets hot and take off when it gets cold." In the fall she passed a group of Barberry bushes, their brilliant red leaves piled under the branches. She collected the leaves and gently traced around them with hand stitches, forming a permanent pile on silk organza in both a memorial to and a celebration of the life cycle. Potential and possibility, learned from nature, are contained in her art.

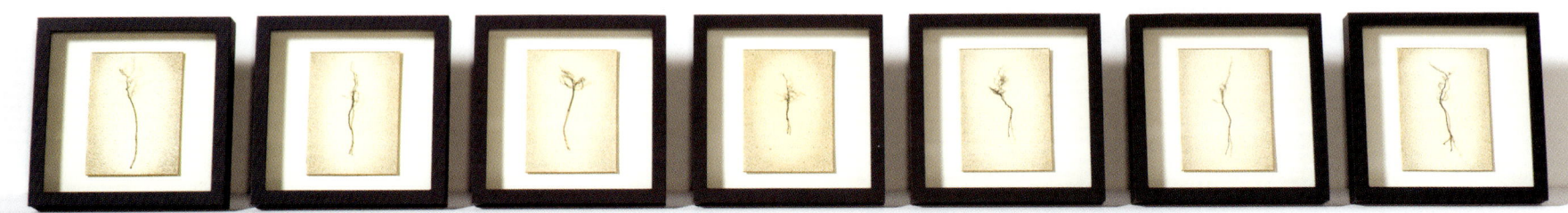

Broken Dream, 2010, 11 x 11 x 2" each, detail right: *Broken Dream*

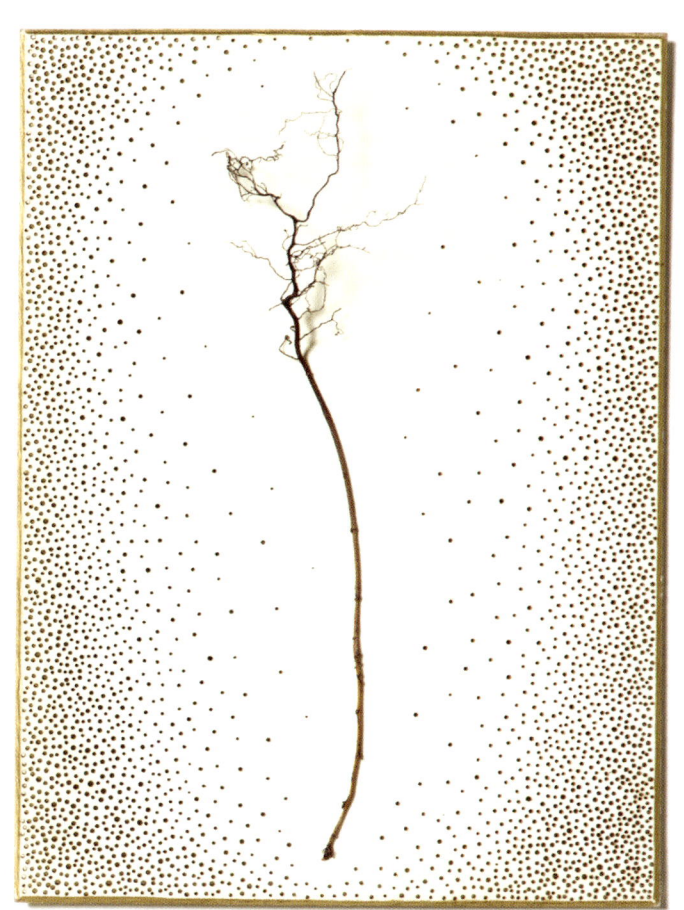
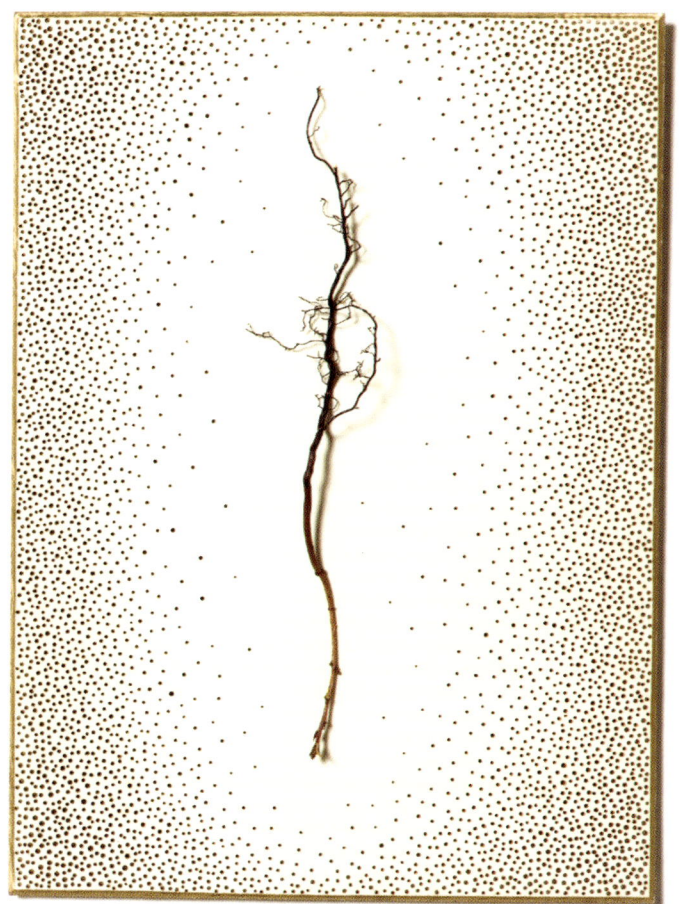

Devorah Sperber's constructions intrigue us by using common materials — spools of thread strung on chains — in an uncommon way. They lure us with assembled pattern, color and form that draws us toward a clear acrylic sphere installed in front of the work. Through the sphere, the spools shrink and condense into pixel-like elements rotated 180 degrees, and coalesce into a familiar image — Grant Wood's *American Gothic*. Sperber writes, "Once the viewer 'sees' the image in the thread, the brain can shift back and forth from focusing on the individual spools to the whole recognizable image." We are prodded to think about what is real, what is subjective, and what is truth.

Sperber chooses iconic images to map in this way: Mona Lisa, Superman, a self-portrait of John Lennon. Grant Wood's vision of Midwestern virtue is an apt reminder of family values issues — the stern father defending his 'not very alluring daughter' — as noted by art critic Robert Hughes.[1] Hughes also points out that the painting was made just after the stock market crash of the late 1920s and the need at the time to focus on what is 'truly American.' The past mingles with our present in this choice. Not only has Sperber turned spools of commercial thread, the materials of the marketplace, upside down but also some of our assumptions about vision, perception, reality and history as well.

[1] Hughes, Robert. 1997. *American Visions: The Epic History of Art in America*, New York: Alfred A. Knopf.

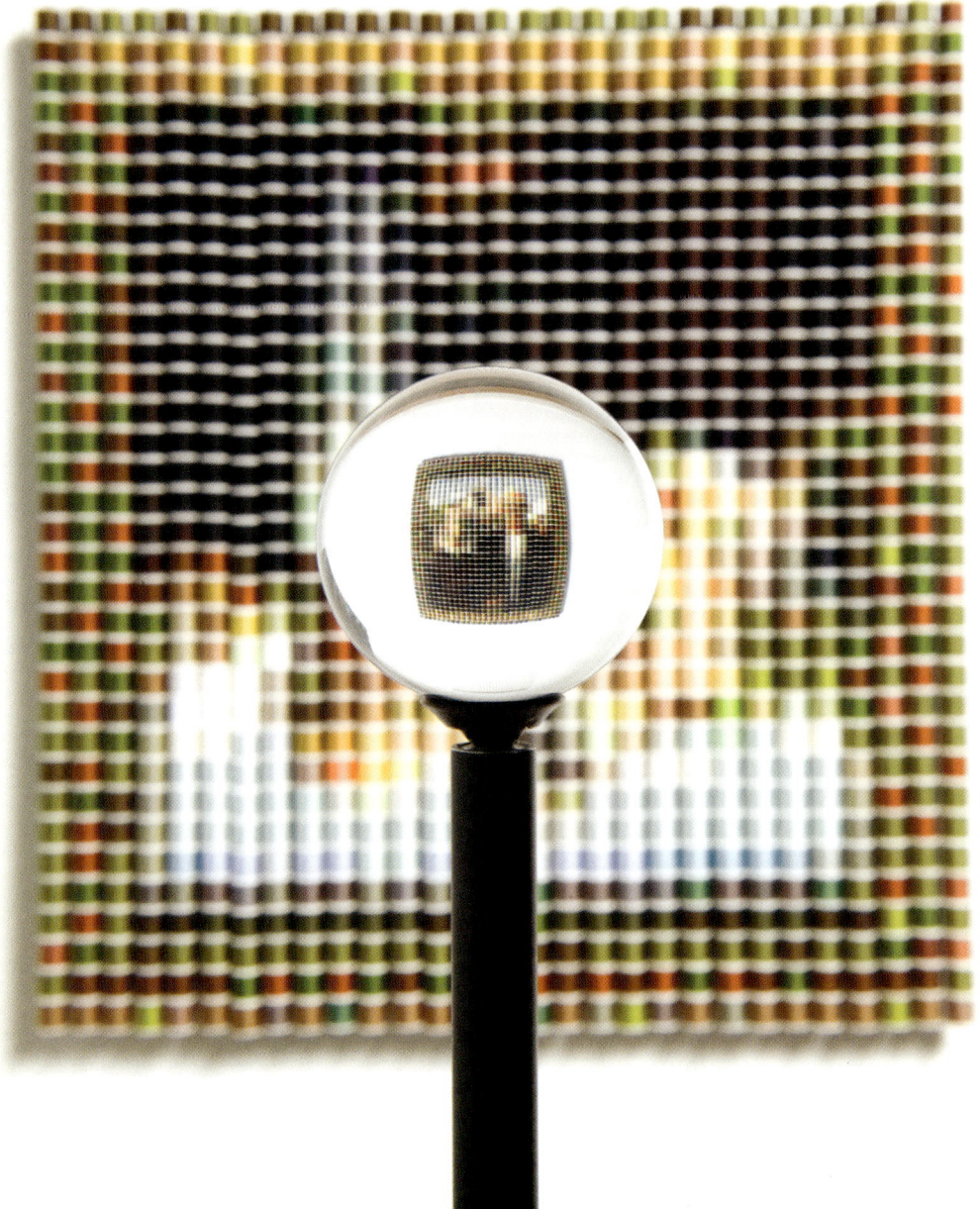

After Grant Wood, American Gothic 2, 2006, 40 x 35.5 x 60"

I am interested in the links between art, science and technology, how the eyes and brain prioritize, and reality as a subjective experience vs. an absolute truth. As a visual artist, I cannot think of a topic more stimulating and yet so basic, than the act of seeing — how the human brain makes sense of the visual world. The brain can only hold or assemble one image at a time, so its initial fixation on the individual thread spools does not allow the recognizable portrait to emerge until the spools are seen through the viewing sphere or from a significant distance. Once the viewer "sees" the image in the thread, he or she cannot erase it. My thread spool installations exemplify my interest in visual perception, the links between art, science and technology through the ages, repetitive processes, truth of materials, the feminist art proposition of bringing genres into "high art," and the scientific systems theory which focuses on the whole as well as its part to gain understanding.

— *Devorah Sperber*

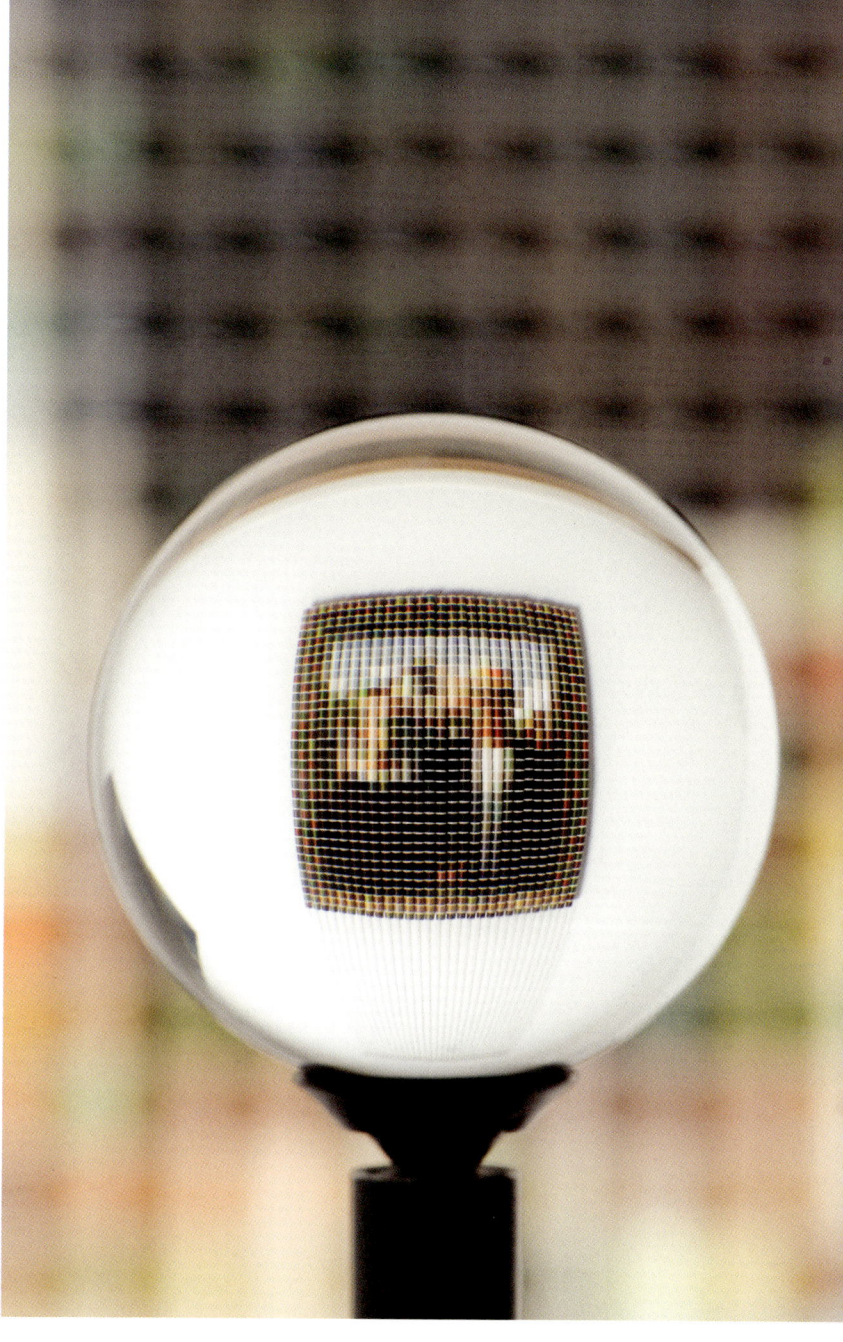

detail: *After Grant Wood, American Gothic 2*

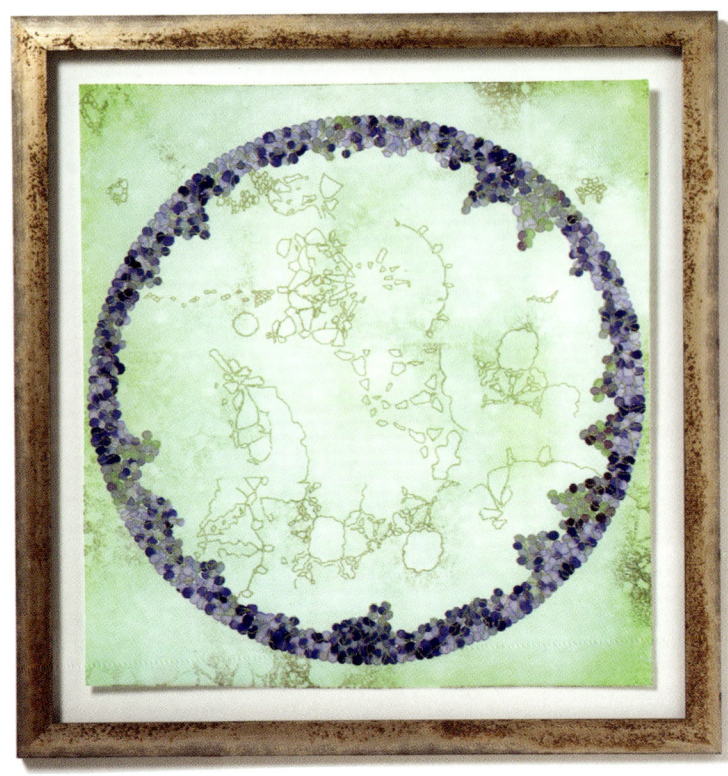

Enhanced Sun Spots, After Galileo, one of three, 2010, 41 x 38.5" each (framed)

Large Regional Still Lives began as a study about personal objects as repositories for memory. I chose several acquaintances and asked them to collect objects that were meaningful to them. I went to each house, arranged the objects into a still life and photographed them. Each object had a compelling story for the owner. This is the second of a three-part work that began with imagery from my own family history and will conclude in the towns where my grandparents were born in Poland and Ukraine.

Another series, *Enhanced Sun Spots, After Galileo,* was generated by a random discovery. While investigating a sun-printing method, I came upon Galileo's drawings of sunspots and was struck by the relationship of the printing method and the drawings.

— *Rachel Brumer*

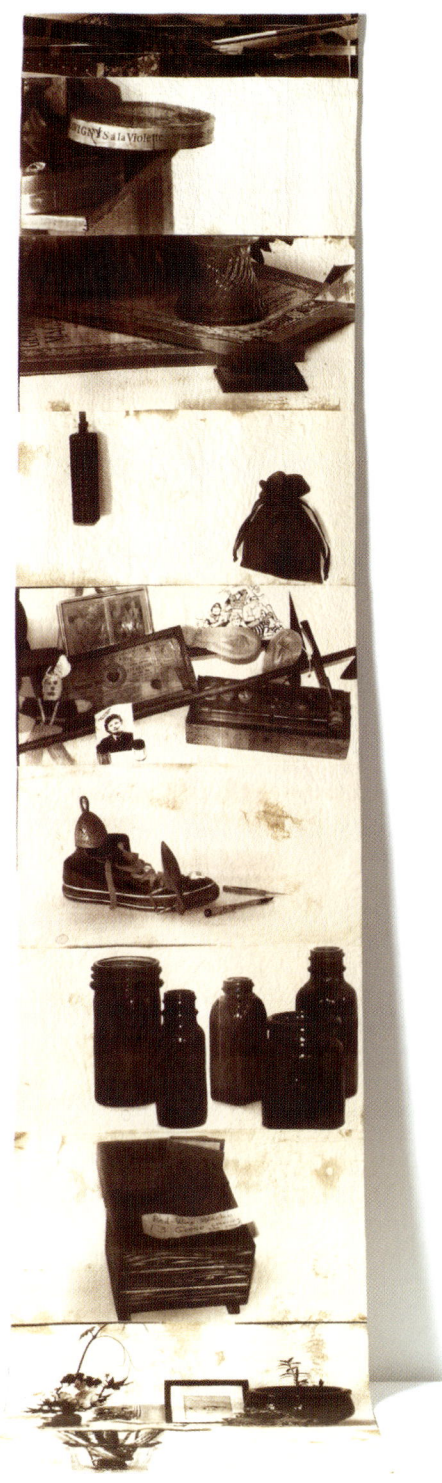

Memory reposes in objects we save. As **Rachel Brumer** prepared for *Large Regional Still Lives*, she pondered: "Why do we have and hold onto objects? What do they mean? When and how do we decide whether to dispose of these objects?"

As she writes in her statement, she was prepared for a variety of interesting choices, but marveled at their accompanying stories. One is a box containing a biographical manuscript that belonged to the owner's mother. Uneasy about what it would reveal, the owner said that she was waiting until her 60th birthday to read it. A stone found at the prison on Robben Island where Nelson Mandela was incarcerated was another memorable possession. Each object became a reminder of a not-so-still life. After photographic reproduction on cloth, these objects become part of a hanging that extends from the ceiling onto the floor, overwhelming in size and suggesting that some objects take on a new and larger-than-life power.

Three smaller, delicate works came about by the 'accidental' discovery of an open mind. Like library card catalogs, almost extant now, the Internet offers a seductive urge to meander into the unexpected. While researching the Vandyke sun-printing process, Brumer came upon Rice University's Galileo Project that showed his drawings of sunspots from 1613. Fascinated with connecting these disparate pieces of information, the sun becomes the focus of a printed, bleached and stitched series. From past to present, Rachel Brumer tracks, reveals and transforms collective memory.

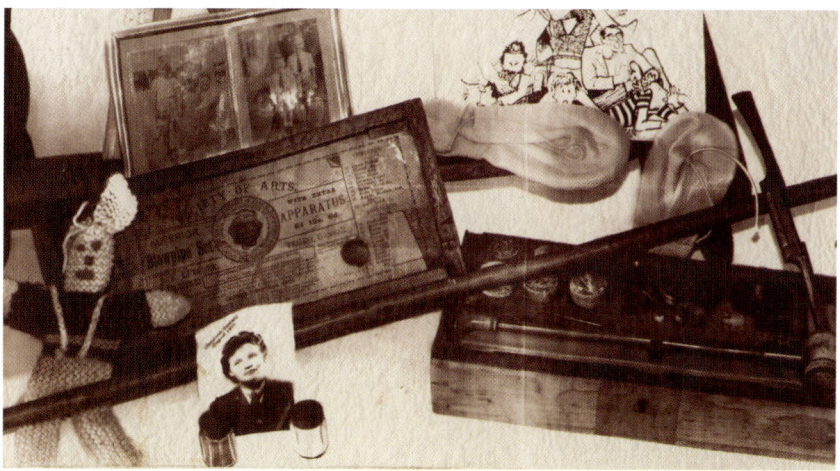

left: *Large Regional Still Lives*, 2010, 204 x 40", above: detail, *Large Regional Still Lives*

45

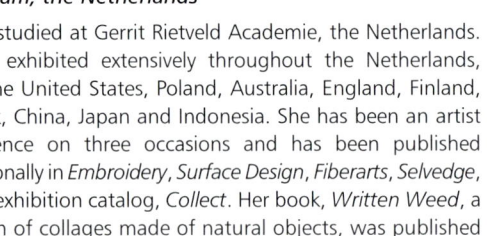

courtesy of the artist

Marian Bijlenga
Amsterdam, the Netherlands

Bijlenga studied at Gerrit Rietveld Academie, the Netherlands. She has exhibited extensively throughout the Netherlands, Japan, the United States, Poland, Australia, England, Finland, Denmark, China, Japan and Indonesia. She has been an artist in residence on three occasions and has been published internationally in *Embroidery*, *Surface Design*, *Fiberarts*, *Selvedge*, and the exhibition catalog, *Collect*. Her book, *Written Weed*, a collection of collages made of natural objects, was published in a limited edition in 2004.

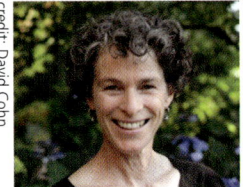

credit: David Cohn

Rachel Brumer
Seattle, Washington

Brumer received her BFA from Mills College, Oakland, CA. She has had three nonverbal careers, first as a professional modern dancer, then as a sign language interpreter, and for the last 19 years as a visual artist. Her art is included in many collections including the Museum of Arts and Design, New York; Seattle Art Museum; Tacoma Art Museum, WA; and Washington State Art in Public Places. Her exhibitions have spanned the country including Oceanside Museum of Art, Oceanside, CA; Seattle Art Museum; and Yeshiva University Museum, New York. In 2009 she received an Artist Trust Fellowship, WA, and was awarded a fellowship at Jentel Artist Foundation in Wyoming. Publications include *Fiberarts, American Craft,* and *Surface Design*.

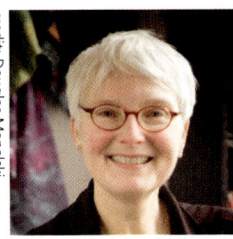

credit: Douglas Manelski

Lou Cabeen
Seattle, Washington

Cabeen is an associate professor at the University of Washington, Seattle, where she has taught since 1993 and serves as chair of the fibers area and co-chair of the School of Interdisciplinary Visual Art. She received an MFA from School of the Art Institute, Chicago, IL, and a BA from the University of Maryland. Select exhibitions include Museum of Arts and Design, New York; Washington Trade and Convention Center, Seattle; Museum of Contemporary Craft, Portland, OR; and Bellevue Arts Museum, Bellevue, WA. Cabeen has also served as guest curator, panelist, and lecturer at multiple venues across the country and internationally. Her work has been included in several publications including *Contemporary Art Quilts* and the exhibition catalog *Conceptual Textiles*, John Michael Kohler Art Center, Sheboygan, WI.

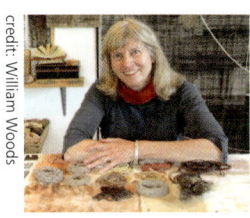

credit: William Woods

Dorothy Caldwell
Hastings, Ontario, Canada

Caldwell, a graduate of Tyler School of Art, Philadelphia, maintains an active international exhibition and teaching schedule. She has pursued research on textile traditions in Japan, India and Australia, and is the recipient of grants and awards including the prestigious Saidye Bronfman Award, 1990, given to one Canadian craftsperson each year. Her work is included in many permanent collections: the Canadian Museum of Civilization, Gatineau, Quebec; The Carlton and Reta Lewis Collection, Washington, D.C.; the Canadian Consulate, Bangkok, Thailand; and the Museum of Arts and Design, New York.

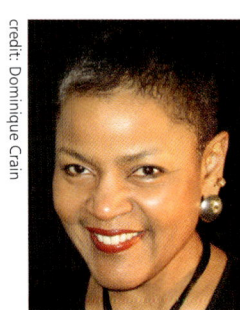

credit: Dominique Crain

Carol Ann Carter
Lawrence, Kansas

Carter is a professor at University of Kansas, Lawrence, Visual Art Department, where she has taught since 1996. She received an MFA from the University of Notre Dame, South Bend, IN, and a BFA from Herron School of Art, Indiana University, Bloomington. She has exhibited across the country with solo and two-person exhibition/video installations including *Mapping Transformation* at Goshen College, Goshen, IN, and *Voices from the Walls*: Video Installation at Kulturforum Bergkloster, Lübeck, Germany. Carter was the recipient of one of five 2010 Lawrence, KS, Arts Commission Phoenix Awards for her activities in art, teaching and the community. Her other honors include a Kansas Arts Commission Individual Artist Fellowship and The Eric Yake Kenagy Lectureship at Goshen College. She has been a selected artist and lecturer both nationally and internationally.

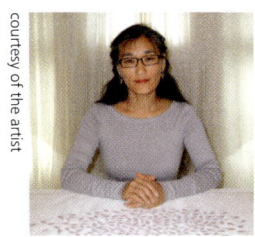

courtesy of the artist

Kyoung Ae Cho
Milwaukee, Wisconsin

Cho has a BFA from Duksung Women's University, South Korea, and an MFA from Cranbrook Academy of Art, Bloomfield Hills, MI. She received the 2006 Wisconsin Arts Board Award Fellowship; 2004 University of Wisconsin-Milwaukee Foundation and Graduate School Research Award; 1997 Lillian Elliott Award; and 1995 Pollock-Krasner Foundation Grant. Cho's works have been shown extensively in venues including Cheonju Craft Museum, Korea; Boulder Museum of Contemporary Art, CO; John Michael Kohler Arts Center, Sheboygan, WI; University of Kentucky Art Museum, Lexington; Clemson University Gallery, Clemson, SC; Snyderman-Works Galleries, Philadelphia; Connell Gallery, Atlanta; Nederlands Textile Museum, Tilburg, the Netherlands; American Cultural Center, Taiwan; University of Hawaii Art Gallery; Detroit Institute of Arts; and the National Museum of Modern Art, Korea. Her work has been reviewed and published in numerous publications including *American Craft*, *Fiberarts*, and *Surface Design Journal*. She is a professor at the University of Wisconsin-Milwaukee.

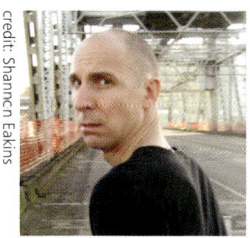

Marc Dombrosky
Las Vegas, Nevada and Dowagiac, Michigan

Dombrosky received an MFA in painting from The Ohio State University and a BFA in painting from the University of Florida, Gainesville. His solo exhibitions include: Portland Art Museum; Platform Gallery, Seattle; Icebox Contemporary, Tacoma, WA; Solomon Fine Art, Seattle; and selected group exhibitions nationally, including the Tacoma Art Museum, WA; Museum of Northwest Art, La Conner, WA; Whatcom Museum of History and Art, Bellingham, WA; d.e.n. contemporary, Los Angeles; PDX Contemporary and Gallery Homeland, Portland, OR; Davidson Contemporary, SOIL Artist Collective, and the Center on Contemporary Art, all located in Seattle. He is currently instructor of art and gallery director at Southwestern Michigan College in Dowagiac, MI, and writes CACBlog for the Contemporary Arts Center in Las Vegas. He is represented by Platform Gallery in Seattle.

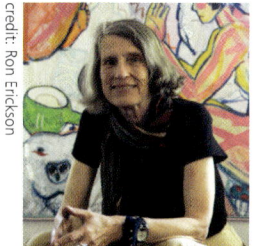

Nancy Erickson
Missoula, Montana

Erickson received her MFA and MA in painting from the University of Montana-Missoula, and a BA in zoology from the University of Iowa, Iowa City. She has participated in some 500 exhibitions from 1965 to present, including most U.S. states, Canada, Mexico, Japan, Korea, the People's Republic of China, Germany, Cape Verde Island, Niger, France, Costa Rica, Burma, New Zealand, and the United Kingdom. She has participated in symposia, and in addition, her work has appeared in many publications, including *Speaking in Cloth: 6 Quilters, 6 Voices*; *Celebrating the Stitch: Contemporary Embroidery of North America*; *The Art Quilt*, and the journals *Fiberarts* and *Camas: an Environmental Journal*, among others.

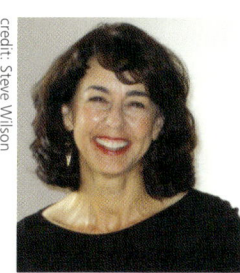

Susan Lordi Marker
Kansas City, Missouri

Marker received an MFA with honors from the University of Kansas, Lawrence. Her work has won awards in the United States and internationally, including Best of Show in the exhibition *Muse of the Millennium*, Seattle Nordic Heritage Museum; Second Prize in *Fiberart International*, Pittsburgh; and International Judges Award in *International Textile Design Competition*, Tokyo. A monograph, *Portfolio Collection: Susan Lordi Marker* was published by Telos Art Publishing. She is one of 10 U.S. artists featured in the book *Art Textiles: USA*. Marker has served on the fiber faculty of both the Kansas City Art Institute and the University of Kansas. She has also created specific works to benefit children's hospitals in Kansas City, Canada and England; the Susan G. Komen organization; and Care for Children in China. In 2005, the alumni organization of University of Missouri, Columbia, awarded her the Outstanding Achievement and Meritorious Service Citation.

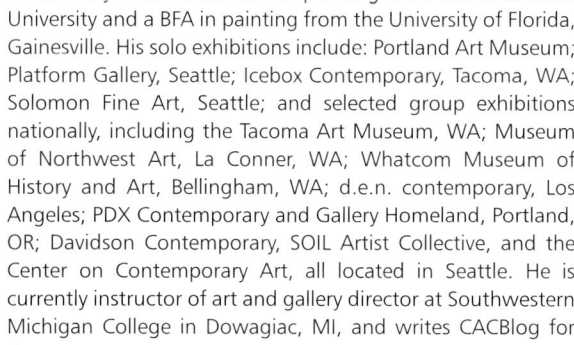

Gail Rieke
Santa Fe, New Mexico

Rieke received her MFA and BFA from the University of Florida, Gainesville. Her art is represented in the permanent collections of the New Mexico Museum of Art, Santa Fe; Albuquerque Museum, NM; Sheldon Memorial Art Gallery, University of Nebraska, Lincoln; Roswell Museum and Art Center, Roswell; University of New Mexico, Albuquerque; and the Santa Fe Institute. Rieke has taught at the University of Florida-Gainesville, the University of Alberta-Edmonton, and the Santa Fe University of Art and Design. She has presented workshops and lectures nationally and internationally. Rieke participated in a six-month retrospective, *Gail and Zachariah Rieke: Found Objects in an Open World* (1999-2000), at the New Mexico Museum of Fine Arts, Santa Fe. She was guest lecturer at the Cheongju International Craft Biennale in Korea in 2007, where she displayed two of her travel journals.

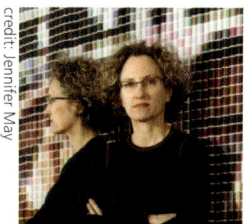

Devorah Sperber
Woodstock, New York

Sperber attended the Art Institute of Colorado, Denver, from 1979 to 1981, and in 1987, she received her BA from Regis University, CO. Sperber has exhibited in numerous institutions nationally and internationally, including the Massachusetts Museum of Contemporary Art (Mass MoCA), North Adams, MA, 2008; the Robert Hull Fleming Museum, University of Vermont, Burlington, 2007; and Montclair Art Museum, NJ, 2004. In 2007, she had a one-person exhibition, *The Eye of the Artist: The Work of Devorah Sperber*, at the Brooklyn Museum of Art, New York. She has been a visiting lecturer or artist across the country including Alfred University, Alfred, NY, and The Graduate Center, City University of New York. Her art is included in the collection of the North Carolina Museum of Art, Raleigh, NC. She was featured on the CBS *Sunday Morning* show in 2009 and her work is published in numerous exhibition catalogs.

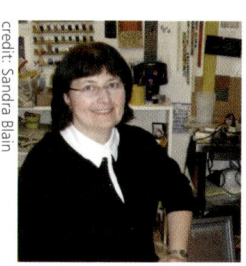

Clare Verstegen
Tempe, Arizona

Verstegen has been a professor at Arizona State University School of Art since 1989. She has an MFA in fiber from Cranbrook Academy of Art, Bloomfield Hills, MI, and a BS in art from the University of Wisconsin-Stevens Point. She has served as an artistic consultant and assistant director at the Arrowmont School of Arts and Crafts, Gatlinburg, TN. Verstegen has exhibited widely across the country. International exhibitions include Korea, Japan, Mexico, and Australia. Her work is in numerous public and private collections. She has contributed to publications including *Fiberarts*, *Surface Design* and *American Craft*.

Exhibition Check List

All works courtesy of the artist unless noted otherwise.

Marian Bijlenga

Japan, 2010
Fish scales, monofilament, machine stitched
23.5 x 23.5"

Congo, 2010
Fish scales, monofilament, machine stitched
23.5 x 23.5"

India, 2010
Fish scales, monofilament, machine stitched
23.5 x 23.5"

Shadow Dots, 2010
Fish scales, monofilament, machine stitched
dimensions variable

Palimpsest 1, 2007
Horsehair, sewing thread, monofilament, machine stitched
106 x 108"
Courtesy of the artist and Cervini Haas Fine Art, Scottsdale, AZ

Rachel Brumer

Large Regional Still Lives, 2010
Vandyke print on hand dyed cotton cloth, machine pieced, hand quilted, cotton thread
204 x 40"

Enhanced Sun Spots, After Galileo, 2010
Vandyke print on hand dyed cotton cloth, discharged, paint, hand embroidered, cotton thread, frame
3 works each 41 x 38.5"

Lou Cabeen

Watershed: Cedar River, 2010
Silk organza, hand stitched, sewing thread
60 x 24"

Watershed: White River, 2010
Silk organza, hand stitched, sewing thread
60 x 24"

Watershed: Snohomish River South, 2010
Silk organza, hand stitched, sewing thread
60 x 24"

September Diary, 2002
Pencil on handmade paper
132 x 89"

Too Late in Asking: A Litany of Loss, 2010
Dyed, discharged, printed fabric, embroidery
16.25 x 38.5" open

Dorothy Caldwell

Fjord, 2010
Resist and discharged cotton, stitching, appliqué
120 x 114"

How Do We Know When It's Night?, 2010
Resist and discharged cotton, stitching, appliqué
120 x 114"

Book of Marks, 2007-2008
Pencil and various inks, notebook
8.5 x 14" open

Carol Ann Carter

Mapping Transformation: Continued…, 2008
Video

Flying Solos, 2010
Video

Arm Bag, 2010
Digital print on paper, frame
24 x 28"

Story Board, 2008
Digital print on paper, frame
24 x 28"

Solo Moments, 2010
Mixed media construction
16 x 80"

Body Objeckte, 2008-2010
Mixed media construction
5 works each 12 x 11 x 3"

Medicine Boxes, 2008-2010
Mixed media construction, wooden box
11 x 14"

Kyoung Ae Cho

Broken Dream, 2010
Roots and burn marks on paper, frame
7 objects each 11 x 11 x 2"

100 Sage Flavored Cubes, 2007
Recycled wild sage leaves, wood, gesso
60 x 60 x 3.5"

Fallen, 2010
Leaves, silk organza, thread
42 x 42"

Marc Dombrosky

His mouth and eyes expressed the double, 2010
Found papers, hand embroidered, cotton thread
Work displayed in two vitrines, dimensions variable
Courtesy of the artist and Platform Gallery, Seattle, WA

Nancy Erickson

Together, 2010
Velvet, paint, machine and hand stitched, quilted
78 x 55"

Caldera, 2010
Velvet, paint, machine and hand stitched, quilted
74 x 64"

The Miracle of a Spring Shower, 2007
Velvet, paint, machine and hand stitched, quilted
71 x 41"

Vigilance, 2007
Velvet, paint, satin, machine and hand stitched, quilted
72 x 42"

Susan Lordi Marker

a remnant: Helianthus, 2010
Linen/polyester blend fabric, gold leaf, dévoré, cloqué, dyed
48 x 84"

The Field is Sown, 2010
Silk, dyed, hand stitched
30 x 48"

Soulskin: Seeding the Prairie, 2000
Iron, copper, nylon, manual cloqué
80 x 42"

Gail Rieke

Blaze of Glory/Japan and Korea, 2007-2009
Found materials, photography, writing, digital print, drawing, paint, collage, quilting, stitching, assemblage, box making, kumihimo braiding
Dimensions variable

Summer Fall Winter Spring, 2008
Mylar, drawings
38" diameter
Box by Sialia Rieke

Devorah Sperber

After Grant Wood, American Gothic 2, 2006
986 spools of thread, stainless steel ball chain and hanging apparatus, clear acrylic viewing sphere, metal stand
40 x 35.5 x 60"

Clare Verstegen

Safety Measures, 2009

Reminders, 2010

Tracing, 2010
Silkscreen on wool felt, heat transfer on wood, burning, basswood, birch plywood
3 works each 18 x 18 x 1.75"

Transition, 2010

Ascent, 2010

Between, 2010

Shifting, 2010

Passage, 2010

Water Level, 2008
Silkscreen on wool felt, heat transfer on wood, burning, basswood, birch plywood
6 works each 10 x 10 x 2.5"